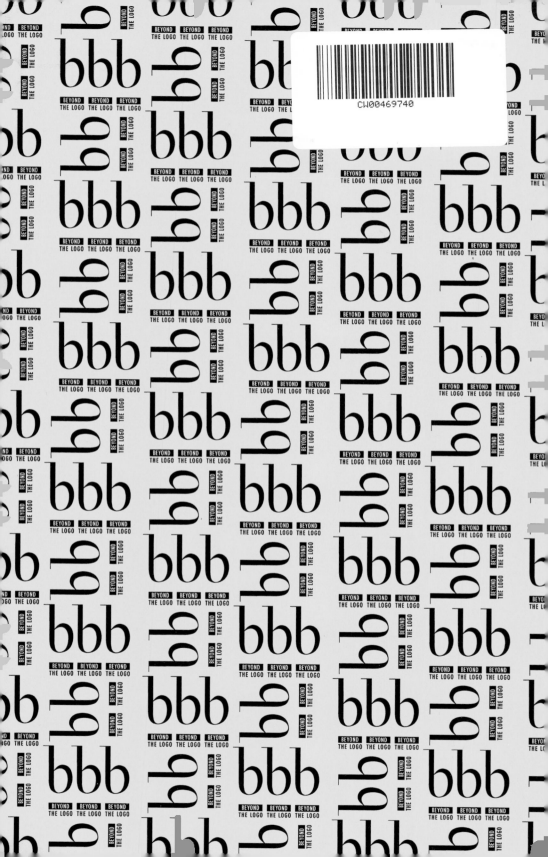

ISBN: 978-0-9575214-0-7

First published in England in 2013
by Beyond Creative Thinking
Copyright © 2011 by
Beyond Creative Thinking

BEYOND THE LOGO:
Creating your brand

By E J Carter

Edited by Sarah Walker
Published by Beyond Creative Thinking

This book is dedicated to:

Mark, Mum & Dad for their support,
inspiration and for simply being there.

A huge thanks to:
Sarah Walker without whom this
book would not have happened.

Becca Hall, for her beautiful illustrations,
and Madeline Ward and Victoria Kitchingman,
for their amazing animations.

THIS BOOK IS POWERED BY AURASMA AUGMENTED REALITY.

I talk about a variety of media in this book - some will be familiar to you and some completely new. I want to bring a few of the examples to life so that you can experience and understand the power of mixing media.

So, with the help of the guys at Aurasma, this book brings you Augmented Reality (AR), where the physical and virtual worlds come together in a rather exciting way!

Throughout the book I'll let you know which images have AR - or you can see page 202 for a list of pages that feature the technology.

DOWNLOAD THE BEYONDCT APP TO BRING THIS BOOK TO LIFE!
(DOWNLOAD THE APP FROM THE APP STORE OR GOOGLE PLAY)

TO DOWNLOAD THE BEYONDCT APP

1 Go to the App store

2 Search for BeyondCT and install the app

3 Open the BeyondCT App, which will take you through a series of startup screens

4 Once the 'camera mode' is activated, hold your smart phone or tablet over the images in this book that have this icon

5 Blue swirls will appear on top of the image to indicate that the file is loading... and then you'll experience the Augmented Reality!

(To view any of the videos full screen, simply double tap the video.)

CONTENTS

A LOGO IS NOT A BRAND
A BRAND IS NOT A LOGO
YOUR BRAND IS 'EVERYTHING'
YOU MUST CREATE A

TOTAL BRAND EXPERIENCE

A LITTLE ABOUT ME AND WHY I DECIDED TO WRITE THIS BOOK

Design has always been a part of my life – it's in my blood – and when I look back at my upbringing, I can really see how I've been influenced by my parents. My dad enjoys working on large engineering projects and figuring out how something can be made to achieve what he wants, which is probably why I like working out the functionality behind things - like the flow of websites or how an event will work. My love of the intricate side of design came from my mum, and I definitely got my determination from her. She's always told us: "do what makes you happy" and "there's no such thing as 'can't'".

I was brought up in the middle of nowhere - the nearest shop, or even pub, was three miles away! - but I wouldn't have wanted it any other way. Having the freedom to explore the fields, make dens and climb trees as a child growing up in the open countryside is probably what started my adventurous side and helped my crazy imagination develop. In the house, I was always the one with my head stuck in a sketchbook, painting or making something, and was the messiest one in the family, usually taking up half of whatever room I was in with my 'stuff'.

I was very lucky with my secondary school, which had a great art department and a dedicated Graphic Design department. That was very rare back then and it wasn't until I went to college that I discovered I was the only one on my course whose school had had this. It was the diversity of art and graphics teachers at my secondary school, and their encouragement, that gave me my foundations. The head of art was fantastic, always encouraging us to experiment with ideas, and one of the other teachers introduced me to typography. She showed me how fonts can really change the look of a design and also introduced me to the world of contemporary graphic design. As a result of her guidance and passion, I was the first student in the school to design a contemporary piece of graphics for A' level.

Although the creative side came naturally, I had to work really hard at everything else. I knew I needed English and Maths GCSEs in order to get into college but those were my worst subjects and, unless you were top of the class, the teachers didn't really care. My maths teacher preferred to spend most of the lesson playing hangman, rather than teaching us anything useful, and my English teachers would be shocked if they knew I was attempting to write a book! Luckily, I've always been stubborn and determined to figure out a solution to any challenge I've faced, so I decided to get some help from private tutors. Through their efforts and my own sheer hard work, I passed English first time and Maths on my second attempt.

I was never the popular 'A star' student, nor was I the lazy drop-out; I was the in-betweener - the one who had ambition but had to work twice as hard as everyone else to achieve my goals. But, rather than seeing that as a negative, I took it as a challenge and loved the constant chase.

Choosing my A' levels was hard, as back then most people only did three, possibly with one extra AS level. I was top of the class in CDT (woodwork) but the Art department wanted me to do Art, Graphics and 3D. I couldn't take four creative subjects, as the practical work would have been too much, so I went with what felt right and took the Art choices – and loved every minute of them.

After school, I went on to take an Art Foundation course at the Cheltenham College of Art and Design, where I had the time of my life, and that was also where I decided that Graphics was really the thing for me. At the time, The Arts Institute at Bournemouth had the best design course outside London, so I enrolled there and learnt about graphic design, layout, printing, web design and motion graphics. It wasn't until some years later, when I took on my first member of staff, that I realised how good my degree course had been. (I'm shocked that students today don't seem to be taught the fundamentals of design any more, such as how to lay out websites and artwork a file for print.)

I left university during the design recession, when interesting junior design jobs were hard to find, so I moved nearer to London and did an internship for a web design/development and print agency - and today they do the development work for my clients! From there I went on to work for a design and marketing company, where I put together and won lots of pitches, but was frustrated because I wasn't allowed to see projects through to completion. I remember being really excited that a client had decided to go ahead with one of my designs, then so disappointed when the printed brochures arrived. My boss had organised the printing and my beautiful brochures arrived printed on high gloss paper, which cheapened the whole look, as gloss paper was completely inappropriate for the brand. I think that was when I became determined to build my own agency, where I could work for myself and have control over projects – but I needed some more experience first.

I went on to better things and was working in Central London for a design agency when I had a phone call from my boyfriend (now husband) to say his company was relocating him to France and did I fancy moving abroad for a few years? Well, I'm always up for a new adventure, so...

Thanks to the contacts I'd built up, I was able to do some freelance work in France and then would travel back to London every few weeks. I went back and forth so much that border security knew me by my first name! France had a different style of graphics to the UK and it was great to soak up this new experience. I was useless at French at school, so got myself a tutor while I was there and he helped me write a mini booklet in French to give to local businesses. I'd pick out businesses I particularly wanted to target, knock on the door and explain to the owner, in my very best French, who I was and what I did. Luckily, most of them were so appalled by my French that they'd switch straight to English, which made my life much easier!

While in France, I was contacted by an agent in London, whose client, Jack Wills, was looking for some design help. At that time they were still a very small company. I got through the first round of interviews, then met with their printer so they could see that I understood the print process and how to artwork a large catalogue. It wasn't until I got the job that it transpired my agent hadn't told them I lived in France! We worked out a deal where I would work on the catalogue from France and pop back to London for meetings, then join them full time when I moved back to the UK at the end of the year.

But, as the end of the year got closer, something in my head was telling me not to do it. I had a chat with Peter Williams, the founder, and explained how I felt: that I wanted my own agency and was going to make or break it within a year. It could have been an awkward situation, but he stuck with me as a freelancer and became my first proper client. And that was the start of my business.

My in-laws' dining room was my first office. From there, I moved it into the spare room in our flat, then, as the business grew, into my first tiny premises across the road. I worked hard, putting in long hours to build up the business, and, eventually, Beyond Creative Thinking became what it is today: an award-winning creative ideas agency with a large office space and clients across a variety of sectors.

HOW I NEARLY LOST IT ALL....

By 2008, I had some great clients and had just turned over my best year. I'd managed to build my business from scratch with my own meagre savings and had never taken a loan from the bank, something I was very proud of. Then the recession hit, and it hit hard.

When money's tight, one of the first things to be cut is marketing and design work. We had a client whose annual budget of £100,000 was slashed to just £20k. Another client, who'd had half a million pounds to spend with us, started getting late with payments. I ended up putting their account on stop several times and racked up huge solicitor's bills fighting for the money. They then went into liquidation and we were third on the debtors list. The day after they went under, they started up again in a different name. As someone who's always strived to be above the line, on time with payments and run my business with integrity, I was furious. It was a painful and expensive experience that taught me a lot about how some people behave when their back's against the wall.

It was a tough time. I remember seeing a statistic in the news that one in three small design agencies was going into liquidation. Existing clients were cutting budgets and potential new clients were putting design projects on hold until things improved or they got additional investment from somewhere.

I'd always kept a reserve account in case something like this should happen, but it was limited and wouldn't tide me over for long. For the first time in my life I was clueless; I had no idea how to get out the other side. Every day I had to go to client meetings and put on a brave face - no one wants to risk investing with a company that looks desperate for business. The media didn't help, spreading doom and gloom about the economy that just made clients go into self-preservation mode. I felt like I was living two lives: in the day I was upbeat to keep team morale high, then I spent my evenings at home wondering how to get out of what felt like a huge black hole that was getting deeper and deeper.

I didn't want to make redundancies, as I was really hopeful things would improve, so I simply cut out all the things the business didn't absolutely need. I didn't pay myself for six months and worked harder than I had ever worked before. I changed the company direction and, most importantly, did what so many others had stopped doing: I consistently invested in marketing and promoting my company. And, eventually, I managed to turn things around without losing any of my staff. It was the toughest time of my life and only those closest to me will ever know what I really went through.

I know that it was worth all that effort and sacrifice because I now have something that I'm very proud of and that gives me immense satisfaction. Having my own business has allowed me to be truly creative, across multiple platforms. I've worked with some amazing businesses and met some great and inspirational people. It's not been easy, but I've experienced and learnt so much more than many of my friends who are also in the design industry.

And I believe the success of my company is down to a combination of these learning experiences and my own natural instinct. Even when I first left university, at a time when digital and traditional print design were kept very separate, I could see that a brand needed to work across all platforms. I knew that someone who was creative could be a good designer, but a great designer would need to be able to work with multiple media and understand how each platform functions in order to maintain brand consistency. And so, as I've built my business, I've made a point of ensuring we have the resources to be able to offer our clients a total brand experience.

WHY I'VE WRITTEN 'BEYOND THE LOGO'

Over the years, I've worked with a variety of brands, all of which have been at different stages of growth. And I've come to notice that a huge number of them - particularly the medium-sized businesses – have one or more of the following in common:

- The owners who are in the early stages of creating a company, think branding is just a logo and take the attitude of 'anything will do', as it's not that important.

- They know what they want their brand to say, where it stands and what the future is, but are confused - do they speak to a website developer or a design agency first? I often hear: 'Surely we can design the website and just stick the logo on afterwards...'

- They don't understand the importance of getting their branding right and what a difference it will make to their success.

- The owners are so busy working on the everyday running of the business that they often don't have time to focus on driving the brand.

- It's a large international brand that has its hierarchy wrong.

- Sometimes an internal member of staff has simply been promoted to handle 'Marketing'. They end up with the responsibility of dealing with design agencies, despite not really knowing what they do, how to properly brief them or even how to effectively utilise their services.

- The brand once worked – or 'did for the time being' when the business started - but the owners have never actually got around to reassessing it or looking at how to make it stronger.

- Internal marketing departments are so caught up in the day-to-day marketing and design of the brand that they don't have either the time to keep up to date and explore new trends or the resources to develop new and fresh ideas.

Does any of that sound familiar?

I know that when these issues are resolved, businesses experience huge leaps in the success of their marketing. Time and again, I've seen strong, consistent and well-executed branding resulting in a higher company profile, increased turnover, accelerated growth and higher profits.

AND YOU DON'T GET ALL THAT FROM JUST A GOOD LOGO

A brand is so much more than a logo and you need to do more than have a good logo and website to satisfy the hunger of your customers in today's market.

So I've created this book to help business owners and marketing departments truly understand how to create a Total Brand Experience. By sharing some 'inside knowledge' on the different creative ways in which you can communicate your brand, giving you tips on how to identify the 'real' designers that will add value to your brand, and explaining how to work with agencies, I hope you'll see how all this can save you time and make you money in the long run.

GO BEYOND THE LOGO TO CREATE AN UNSTOPPABLE ORGANISATION!

AND, BY THE WAY...

Being a busy creative and business owner means I don't tend to read books that are large enough to be a door stop. So I've made sure this book is small enough that you don't get bored, but big enough that it gives you lots of brilliant information and helpful hints and tips so you understand the Total Brand Experience. I've also included lots of pictures to keep the left side of your brain working!

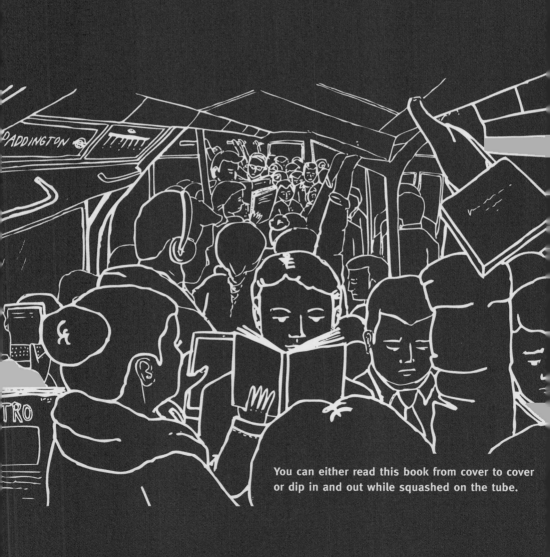

You can either read this book from cover to cover
or dip in and out while squashed on the tube.

WORKING WITH EMMA ENABLED US
TO MOVE OUR CATALOGUE AND ENTIRE
BRAND FORWARD. SHE SURPASSED OUR
ALREADY-HIGH EXPECTATIONS IN EVERY
AREA, FROM A COMPLETE REDESIGN OF
OUR CATALOGUE, TO OUR 'IN THE ALPS'
LOGO, POSTERS, DIRECT MAIL PIECES
AND INTERNAL COMMUNICATIONS.
SHE IS PASSIONATE ABOUT WHAT SHE
DOES AND HAS A GREAT EYE FOR DETAIL.
I WOULD CERTAINLY RECOMMEND HER.

PETER WILLIAMS, FOUNDER OF JACK WILLS

SECTION ONE:
ESTABLISHING YOUR BRAND

WHAT IS A BRAND?

A BRAND IS NOT A LOGO; IT IS AN ORGANISATION, PRODUCT OR SERVICE THAT DELIVERS A PROMISE AND A FEELING. A BRAND DEMONSTRATES 'WHO' AN ORGANISATION IS, COMMUNICATES ITS BELIEFS AND CORE VALUES AND KNOWS HOW TO CONNECT WITH ITS AUDIENCE. A BRAND NEEDS TO TELL A STORY AND DRIVE ITS BIG IDEA FROM THE CORE.

BRANDING RUNS THROUGH THE ENTIRE ORGANISATION, FROM HOW THE PHONE IS ANSWERED, TO WHAT PAPER THE LITERATURE IS PRINTED ON, TO THE TONE OF VOICE USED IN SOCIAL MEDIA, AND SO ON.... YOUR BRAND IS YOU.

BUILDING A TOTAL BRAND EXPERIENCE

I always talk to clients about their branding in terms of what they want their customers to experience – and by customers, I mean not only the people buying the product or service, but also anyone who 'buys into' their business: employees, suppliers, associates and affiliates.

Every aspect of your brand needs to be appropriate for its market and live up to its promise, or you will lose trust and the brand will falter. If you're a large corporate, this can be incredibly detrimental to your business.

> ## A BRAND FOR A COMPANY IS LIKE A REPUTATION FOR A PERSON.
>
> JEFF BEZOS, FOUNDER OF AMAZON

ADVERTS. RADIO.
EVENTS
TV
PAY PER CLICK
EXHIBITION STANDS.
online
Banner
Augmented Reality
FACEBOOK.
MAGAZINES
BILLBOARDS.
APPS
ADVERTISING.
projection mapping...
QR CODE
DIGITAL CHANNELS
BRANDED MERCHANDISE
Social media
BRANDED SCENTS
VIDEO
PACKAGING
STORE AND OFFICE BRANDING.
EMAIL CAMPAIGN.
Printed collateral
BROCHURE
Stationary
DIRECT MAIL
WEBSITE DESIGN.
competitors
WHAT TYPE OF BRAND
WHAT
Design.
LOGO
YOU
BRAND
Tone Of Voice
BRAND ARCHITECTURE

Putting a brand together is a bit like constructing a building. First you have a plan (the product or service you're selling and an idea of who you want to be selling it to), then you lay the foundations (brand hierarchy, tone of voice, values, image, clear target market, etc.). As the brand grows, the more experiences you add and, over time, your plan takes shape and is realised. The tools and experiences may change during the life of the build, but the foundations remain the same.

PAPER
STOCK
Illustration

BRANDING, THEN AND NOW

Back when life was simple... After the Second World War, the 'rise' of mass-produced consumer goods began changing the way we thought and shopped. Back then, a brand simply needed a healthy advertising campaign to succeed. Supermarkets made it easy for consumers to get their hands on the latest products, which, in turn, made it easier for companies to sell their products. This straightforward way of buying and being sold to was a new experience for consumers and they lapped it up. Life was sweet for the advertisers and producers.

At that time, advertising was simply aimed at the end consumer and, because people were so hungry for these new brands, the companies behind them drove messages of 'how this product will enhance your life'; people bought them - and bought them in their millions. Everyone was happy: the companies made lots of money, people believed their lives were being enhanced and some of the biggest advertising agencies we know today were born.

Unlike now, there wasn't much choice in the way of media back then, and socio-economic groups (your As, Bs and Cs, etc.) were much simpler. This made it far easier than it is today, to launch a product, get in the face of the consumer and be successful.

NOW...

A brand needs to be far more in tune with its audience and much more 'transparent'. With the rapid rise of digital media, which has given both businesses and individuals the ability to reach huge audiences at the push of a button on a phone, and news corporations fighting for the next big scandal, everyone in business needs to be very careful about how they present themselves and what they say.

The Body Shop was one of the first to get caught out in such a public way and hauled over the coals for not living up to its reputation. The business presented itself as 'caring and ethical' and Anita Roddick, founder of the brand, claimed it was, 'the most honest cosmetics company in the world'. With the help of the media, Roddick was put on a pedestal and her personal brand launched full throttle. It's been reported that Roddick got carried away, fabricating stories about how and why she started The Body Shop and stressing that the products were natural, ethical and not tested on animals. But when journalists, most notably Jon Entine at the Daily Mail, started uncovering the truth behind the image, Roddick found out that enthusiasm and charisma were no substitute for honesty and integrity. As her version of the truth started being questioned, the lies continued and the truth was manipulated. A notable example is The Body Shop's changing of their trademark phrase from 'Not Tested on Animals' to 'Against Animal Testing', after it was revealed that most of the ingredients in their products were, in fact, tested on animals. And it appeared that, rather than cleaning up their act, the company chose to defend themselves against attacks on their ethics, values and integrity by issuing legal threats.

Roddick was accused of a number of unethical business practices, including the exploitation of the Brazillian Kayapo Indians. In 1994, an article by Jon Entine was published in the US magazine, Business Ethics, detailing contradictions between The Body Shop's public image and the truth. Two years later, Jon's article, 'The Queen of Bubble Bath', revealed that the level of supposedly beneficial botanical extracts was so microscopic as to be ineffective and that they were mixed with so many petrochemicals that the products were no better than any other ordinary high street product. It also uncovered that, while the brand claimed to give an inordinate amount of pre-tax profits to charity, it had, in fact, given nothing to charity over its first 11 years and far less than the average company over its entire history. Despite telling the public that Fair Trade was the 'cornerstone' of the company, The Body Shop's own statistics showed it represented a mere 0.16% of total turnover. The article also reported that sweatshops had been used to create some of the products... and the truth of the 'real' Body Shop was out there for the public to see.

An article in the Guardian reported that Roddick had previously attacked L'Oreal for employing only 'sexy' women on its sales counters and for testing on animals, yet, in 2006, she sold The Body Shop to them. That led to animal protection groups calling for a boycott of the chain. Consumers hate to be taken for granted and once their trust is abused, it's gone forever.

I believe that if The Body Shop had truly been what it claimed, or if Roddick had tried to make things right, the brand would be very different today. When I was younger, The Body Shop used to sit proudly on the high street and was known as a company that was different from others, with better values. But, today, it's just 'there', with the same branding and slightly dated packaging, looking as though it's stuck in a time warp, which is never good for a brand. When was the last time you purchased something from one of their stores?

The sad truth is that, had Roddick acted with integrity, the company could have still been up there, recognised and admired for standing by its beliefs and making a difference, instead of being thought of as just another brand that took advantage of its customers. The story of The Body Shop serves as a lesson about the consequences of abusing your brand.

It's important to recognise that consumers are more complicated and educated than they used to be. They don't just want good products and services; they want a brand that has real values and stands for something they can associate with, that tells the truth and shows personality. This is why it's so important to understand the different platforms a brand can use to create 'The Experience'. We see millions of logos every day, but how many do we remember? The ones that stay in our memories and become part of our lives are the ones that are more than 'just' a logo; they are the ones that have taken the time to really get to know their audience and understand how to interact effectively on a two-way level.

Just look at some of the young people who wear Jack Wills clothing. They're not just wearing a t-shirt with the Jack Wills logo on it; they're making a statement about who they are, who they hang with and the lifestyle they want to lead. They follow the brand, they 'live and breathe it', not just by wearing the clothes but by interacting with the brand and the brand giving back to them. It's not simply about pushing advertising out there anymore; you need to interact on every level, from print to digital to hands-on, face-to-face experiences.

Jack Wills is also very good at telling the story of the brand's history – they hone in on their brand's core truth and amplify it. This then attracts followers who are looking for that 'something' that somehow shows the world who they are.

The rise of blogging and social media sites has made it even easier for consumers to voice their opinions and bad experiences and, let's face it, the media much prefers a story on a brand's demise to one on a great success. We live in ruthless times and any company not sticking to their morals and values and not being open and honest will get slaughtered, both in the broadcast and print media and online. 'The Consumerist', which gives consumers (and ex-employees!) a platform on which to share their positive and negative experiences about how companies interact with their consumers, is one of the most popular blogs on the internet, and all those reviews – good and bad - can be seen by the whole world at the click of a button.

> **ONE REASON THIS CONSUMER-LED RETRIBUTION HAS BECOME SO POPULAR IS THAT IT IS MUCH EASIER TO ATTACK A FACELESS COMPANY THAN A REAL PERSON.**
>
> **ROHIT BHARGAVA, PERSONALITY NOT INCLUDED, 2008**

Branding has had to change because we, as consumers, have changed. Towards the end of the chapter I'll talk more about how to make sure yours isn't one of those 'faceless' companies.

BRAND ARCHITECTURE

This is about the 'foundations' I mentioned earlier. The architecture should clearly show what's driving your brand, i.e. what the brand is representing and what its purpose is. Is it one main overarching brand, such as Virgin? Do you have several brands that are endorsed by the Group Name or do you treat each product as a different brand and drive each one separately, as Diageo (owners of Guinness, Smirnoff and Moet & Chandon, among others) does? You can then add an extra layer to some of these brands and target different markets within them...there are a lot of different options, but you must take the time to define the architecture for your brand, so that you can:

■ Clearly see what direction the company is going in

■ See how future decisions – such as acquisitions - might affect each area of the business and how you can best incorporate these into your architecture, e.g. will they be consumed by the main brand, endorsed or separate?

■ See if just one core message is needed (if it's pushing a single brand) or whether different messages and teams are needed (if it's pushing several individual or sub-brands)

■ See how many ways a marketing, design, or new product development budget might need to be split. Is it one way or several?

If you're just starting your business, spend some time working on your brand's architecture, as this will help clarify the direction in which you push the company. It will also help marketers or designers that you speak to understand what needs to be considered.

If you have already established your company, hopefully you will have your brand architecture in your brand manual. In reality, most of the recently-established companies I've spoken to haven't even thought about it, so if that's you, you're not alone! Perhaps now this is something you - or a small team within your business - can work on.

If you're a medium to large company and you either have nothing in place or the company has grown in different directions over the years through acquisitions, divisions, etc., then you may want to bring in a brand expert to work with you and your team. Brand architecture tends to be more complicated if several acquisitions have taken place and you're left with a variety of products and services.

THE MAIN TYPES OF BRAND ARCHITECTURE

The brand architecture of most organisations generally falls into one of four categories:

1. CORPORATE OR MONOLITHIC: THE SINGLE BUSINESS IDENTITY

The organisation uses one name and one visual system to communicate, for example: Apple, Yamaha, British Airways and Heinz. The emphasis is on branding the company so that the customer's overall attitude towards the company will transfer into their feelings about its individual product lines.

Yamaha uses the same logo (single business identity) to represent all its products, which include pianos, guitars, and even motorcycles.

Heinz is not only recognized by the name but also by its iconic symbol - or keystone - so if you take the name away it's still recognised as being Heinz.

Apple is not only widely loved, but its brand architecture is quite brilliant. It evolved from a pure computer company called 'Apple Computer, Inc.' to simply being called 'Apple'. Changing the name was a deliberate move to signify that it was no longer just a computer company, but a digital entertainment, creativity and communication company or, as Steve Jobs described it, 'a mobile devices company'. Each product has several strands which link it back to the main brand, creating a 'virtuous circle', where the extension benefits from the brand, the brand benefits from the extension

and the Apple stores allow the whole range to be presented together, strengthening the brand: 'Apple'. The products have a simple naming structure and such coherent brand identity linking them to the main brand that you cannot class its products as sub-brands.

Advantages: This enables all the focus to be on the 'one brand' rather than diluting the focus/budgets across several brands.

Disadvantages: If one of the products or services fails, it can tarnish the entire brand.

2. ENDORSED: THE MULTIPLE BUSINESS IDENTITY

The organisation owns a variety of brands, each of which is endorsed by the group name or visual style, for example, Nestlé.

Endorsed brands are usually grown through the acquisition of suppliers, competitors, etc., who each have their own name, culture and reputation. This has the potential to cause confusion, but it is absolutely essential that, in acquiring a competitor's business, the brand being acquired is not destroyed.

One example is Nestlé's acquisition of Rowntree, which owned a lot of different well-known product brands, including Kit Kat. Nestlé therefore kept the individual product brands but got rid of the parent Rowntree brand.

I only ever associated Rowntree with Fruit Pastilles - a Kit Kat was simply a Kit Kat – and this is probably down to the fact that, while Fruit Pastilles were widely advertised as 'Rowntree's Fruit Pastilles', the Kit Kat wrappers I remember only had Rowntree on the back.

When Nestlé started stamping their logo on the front of the Kit Kat wrapper, because Rowntree never had, it just looked like they were saying 'we own this brand now'. That one branding decision has probably made them look a bit like a 'monopoly' corporate, which is not what today's consumers want. I just hope this doesn't happen to our much-loved brand, Cadbury, now that they've been acquired by Kraft!

Advantages: This allows a corporation to dominate a space in a specific sector, such as confectionary. It also allows each brand they acquire to keep its own identity that the audience is already familiar with and loyal to.

Disadvantages: If the organisation becomes greedy and starts buying up lots of well-known brands that the public love, they could easily be seen as one big superpower trying to monopolise an industry. That could destroy public opinion, because people don't want to buy from faceless giants.

3. BRANDED: THE BRAND-BASED IDENTITY

This is where the organisation owns a number of brands or companies that are apparently unrelated, both to each other and the corporation, such as Diageo, Unilever and P&G.

DIAGEO

Advantages: This enables the organisation to move into different and new sectors with some of their brands, without affecting the other brands. If one brand fails it is highly unlikely to negatively impact the others.

Disadvantages: You need to have sufficient resources to handle several brands in completely different sectors.

A brand will generally fall into one of the three core categories above. I use the word 'generally' because when you delve deeply into a brand's architecture, especially when dealing with large corporations, the main core elements have often been extended to give even further clarity and understanding to the hierarchy:

4A. THE CORPORATE BRAND CAN HAVE A 'GRADUATION' OR 'SUB-BRAND'.

The corporation instils its values and ethics across the entire company in the same way as the 'Corporate Brand' model, but the graduation or sub-brands not only make the main corporate brand stronger, they enable the brand to appeal to a wider audience.

BMW also uses graduation to appeal to a variety of audiences, for example, the BMW 1 series is aimed at young professionals, whereas the BMW 640i is aimed at executives. They are very different audiences but this sub-branding means BMW doesn't have to rely on one particular market being buoyant and can grow its brands across different target markets.

American Express has a consistent message across the organisation - 'Don't leave home without it' - yet there are different graduations of the brand, such as the 'gold' and 'black' cards. The customer isn't buying into the brand because it meets their needs, as with BMW; it's purely a status symbol or ego boost. AmEx is simply rewarding people for their level of buy-in with a different coloured card! It's incredible that such a simple thing as giving someone a different coloured card can have such an impact, but that's the power and beauty of branding and customers absolutely love it. We all like feeling special, so see if you can tap into the idea - it's what every brand should be striving for.

4B. THE CORPORATE BRAND CAN ALSO HAVE AN 'EXTENSION' OR 'COMBINED BRAND'. I ALSO OFTEN REFER TO THIS AS AN 'UMBRELLA BRAND'.

This allows for different brand values to be added to each new service or product. The corporate brand acts as the core foundation or 'umbrella', giving credibility, and the product or service brand defines the target market. For example, Kellogg's is the core foundation and Frosties or Special K defines the target market. Both the product brand and the company brand benefit from the association.

AND... some corporations use the brand-based system for the core of the corporation and then different systems for their individual brands. Unilever is a great example of this...

Under the 'branded' hierarchy, they have individual brands, including: Lipton, Knorr, Comfort, Wall's and Domestos. These are apparently unrelated brands and operate very independently in the market.

But by also using the 'combined brand hierarchy', their Wall's brand, which is trusted by millions, has Magnum, Cornetto and Carte D'Or. Both brand names support and endorse each other, creating a very strong product.

However, the Wall's brand has not been combined with the ice cream brand Ben & Jerry's, which Unilever also owns, as this was an independant company that Unilever bought in 2000. As it was already such a strong brand on its own, the association with Wall's wouldn't have added any benefit; it could have caused confusion and damaged the Ben & Jerry's brand.

This hierarchy enables Unilever to own individual brands but also to launch new products that piggyback on already trusted brands, making entry to the market easier and more successful.

Brand Architecture - things to think about:

- Does your company have a clear architecture?
- Is your brand structured in a way that allows all of your activities to operate to their fullest potential?
- Is there confusion between any of your brands' names?
- Is your brand creating the right impression?

JOINT VENTURES

Finding other brands that you can partner with can result in some exciting new developments and can help both brands to not only grow but also gain new customers outside their usual target market. Nike and Apple brought exercise and music together by developing the Nike+, which allowed footwear to wirelessly communicate with an iPod. Nike+ grew users by 50% in 2011, to over five million.

BRANDING TEAMS AND GUARDIANS

Larger organisations tend to have dedicated teams working on each brand. These teams can vary in size: sometimes they will consist of several marketing and communications specialists; sometimes there will be in-house designers and other times this is outsourced, or there is a mixture of in-house and outsourcing. Mars, for example, have dedicated teams for each separate product, which gives them a greater level of focus. However, this approach can cause problems if a particular project arises where multiple brands are involved. Cross-communication is needed to ensure each brand is fully understood, so the approval process is often longer.

I experienced this problem recently, when I was working on a project with a large brand, because the main point of contact did not understand the other brands involved. As a result, I had to work with the individual heads of marketing for each brand, who all had different understandings of the project in hand. The lack of communication and organisation between these key people resulted in the project taking over twice as long as it should have, almost missing the deadline. Of course, we worked round the clock for them, but costs and stress could have been greatly reduced with a simple bit of organisation and them taking the time to understand simple things, such as what a high-res file is!

For small and medium-sized companies I believe that keeping it small and having an agreed objective and common understanding from the offset is key. For example, a few years ago I worked on a branding project for a data centre, in a team consisting of the two company Directors - who both had the same vision - a marketing expert and me. We all brought something different to the table and it worked really well. The result was the completion of a series of very successful projects, including the launch of their new data centre.

I can't stress enough that the people within a team need to have the same understanding about the brand's goal. I've worked with small companies who have done the right thing in appointing a key team of decision makers but have then discovered that, as a team, they find it difficult to make decisions because they all have different ideals and goals.

If you're a small company, it's a good idea to appoint a 'brand guardian' – someone who ensures the brand is kept consistent across all media and that brand guidelines (which I'll talk about in Chapter 4) are adhered to. This can be someone internal or, if you have a long-standing relationship with your design agency, you could appoint them. If it's a designer that's appointed, then they can take responsibility for making decisions on when exceptions can be made with the brand. For example, recently a client was trialling a possible new division of their business, which would appeal to a different target market, although it still needed support from the publicly familiar main brand. So, rather than following the exact guidelines for the main brand, selected elements were used to give the new division the overall brand association and familiarity it needed.

GUARDIANS

The brand guardian can also help ease the daily pressure on the MD or Directors by being the point of contact for both internal staff and external teams when they have a query over any aspect of branding. Questions often get answered and small problems resolved more quickly if teams don't need to bother the people right at the top of the organisation with issues that might be considered trivial in the grand scheme of things.

Brand guardians are particularly useful if you are a franchisor. I was appointed Brand Guardian for one of our clients a few years ago and one thing I noticed was that, because they were growing at such a fast rate, the founders and head of marketing didn't have time to brief new staff on what could and couldn't be done with the brand. Although there was a set of brand guidelines in place, the document was often forgotten about and, as we all know, there's no substitute for being able to pick up the phone and ask, "Can I...?", or knowing you can quickly email over a graphic that's been designed and say, "It doesn't look quite as it should, how can I fix it?"

GET YOUR STAFF ON BOARD AND GROW

As I mentioned at the start of this chapter, the way we work and interact with brands has changed. A brand with a strong sense of purpose, ethics and personality is what really attracts consumers today, and businesses are finding success from being both commercially and socially minded, rather than focusing purely on the bottom line and shareholder value.

In order to really connect with consumers and make sure they see the people behind the organisation, you need the core values to run throughout your company. There's little point in the top management setting values and a direction for the business unless the whole team understands them and really works in accordance with them, as a team.

You need to instil the passion for your brand right at the beginning, then, as you grow, it will become second nature to everyone. If you're a large organisation and want or need to implement a dramatic change of direction, it can be time-consuming and quite a drain on resources. However, if you've already done all you can to make sure passion and loyalty for the brand runs strongly throughout the company and have explained the changes properly to your staff, making those changes will be embraced and the staff will back your decisions.

Many people believe large corporations are faceless - and most are! – but that's usually because they were faceless to start with, rather than having become faceless over time. These types of corporations are generally the ones that have focused purely on the bottom line and have failed to understand and embrace how consumers' behaviour and needs have changed. Passion and vision must run through a company right from the start to make sure those core values continue to flow as the company grows. When that's done well, success is virtually assured. Look at Apple and Google - they are huge but still have the same passion, vision and personality that was instilled by their founders in the beginning, which is probably why we, as consumers, love the brands so much.

I've had the great pleasure of working with Jack Wills, where every member of staff lives and breathes the brand. Walking into the office is like walking into a big family, which results in a great working atmosphere that resonates right through their in-store staff and on to the customers. If you can cultivate this kind of enthusiasm for your brand, it will come across when all the people who interact with the brand – staff, customers, suppliers and affiliates - are talking to friends or using social media.

I also think it's important to allow staff to help write blogs for the company website, or the odd press release. They'll feel that their opinion is valued and it also means that more content is being pushed out into the media. You'll be surprised at what giving your staff their few seconds of fame can do for their morale - and that quiet person in the corner may well surprise you!

If you truly work as a team, you can create a really powerful Total Brand Experience.

DON'T FORGET TO HAVE FUN WITH YOUR BRAND!

Getting your brand architecture in place will take some time and effort and you might be thinking, 'I don't want to lay out a plan, I just want to get on with it. I don't care about the architecture, I know what we're doing and the direction we're going in...I just want to have fun and build our brand, products and services.'

That's understandable, but I'm not saying brand planning has to be boring - far from it, I'm a creative thinker and do-er myself! What I'm saying is that it's necessary to get the foundations firmly bedded down first so every current and new member of staff knows who the brand is, how it's structured and it

GOOGLE HAS BECOME THE WORLD'S MOST ICONIC SEARCH ENGINE THANKS TO THOUSANDS OF EXPERIMENTS.

WOLFF OLINS GAME CHANGERS RESEARCH, 2011

doesn't feel like a jumbled mess. If you're a small to medium-sized company it should be relatively quick to map out.

Once the foundations are set, you can really start to have fun and be creative. Maybe think about having an 'ideas board', where you can park any crazy ideas that pop up along the way and come back to them at a later date to decide whether they're worth trying. You could even create a system that supports experimental behaviour among employees, like Google, who allow staff one day a week to pursue their own projects. This is how AdSense and Gmail were created.

IN SUMMARY...

A large part of the strength of your business comes from the strength of your brand, so you must make sure that your brand's vision and beliefs run through the entire organisation. Doing this consistently and ensuring all your staff portray the right message will help create a great team spirit and will make your brand more powerful. Remember that customers want and expect more in today's market. Getting the foundations right will not only help build trust, but will also help you attract customers who believe in the same values. And relationships built on trust and shared values are the ones that last.

NEVER UNDERESTIMATE THE IMPORTANCE OF YOUR BRAND.

UNDERSTANDING YOUR AUDIENCE AND YOUR BRAND

YOUR AUDIENCE IS YOUR CUSTOMER BASE, AND ONLY BY UNDERSTANDING THEM WILL YOU BE ABLE TO DECIDE ON THE RIGHT MIXTURE OF PLATFORMS TO USE TO CREATE YOUR UNIQUE TOTAL BRAND EXPERIENCE.

In a world that's more connected than ever, it's vital to understand who your customers are and where they are. Although I'm no marketing expert or customer analyst, I need to know about a client's customer base in order to create inspiring, creative ideas that they will understand and respond to. Any creative agency you work with - whether digital, traditional or multi-disciplined - will need to know as much as possible about your target audience.

Customers expect a brand to work hard to keep them happy, which means understanding their needs and wants, then giving them those things. One brand that made a name for itself based on working hard for its customers was First Direct (the first phone-only banking company). They had a system in place where if a customer phoned into the call centre in the middle of the night needing information or approval on a mortgage and none of the staff on that shift could handle the case, there would be an appropriate member of staff 'on call' who would drive into the office. First Direct understood that being involved in large financial transactions can be stressful – especially when it's something like a mortgage for a person's home – so they did their best to make sure that their customers could get answers and service as quickly as possible, even outside normal working hours. With today's technology, this could have been sorted from home, but it shows the level of service some companies are prepared to rise to - and this is one of the reasons the First Direct brand is still popular.

People buy from people and the growing number of social media sites means that companies have more opportunities to interact with their customers and for those customers to interact with potential new customers, and so on... There are a lot of companies sending out messages all the time, a huge percentage of which get deleted before they've even been read, so you need to be as specific as you can in your targeting, and that means gaining a much deeper understanding of your audience than you needed to ten years ago.

You need to research your current and potential clients and find out what interests them, where they're based, what social media they use (Twitter, LinkedIn, Facebook, etc.) and what time of day they tend to be online.

You could get a small team together to research what people are saying on social media and when they are saying it. Perhaps a short questionnaire could be sent out to existing customers with an incentive for completing and returning it.

We compiled such a survey for BlueSquare Data Centre. In return for filling out the questionnaire, customers were entered into a prize draw and the winner was then announced in the paper, with a photograph of them holding the prize. This not only gave the Data Centre vital information about their customers, but also created some positive PR. The person who won was over the moon, as he'd never won anything before, so it created a stronger bond between the company and that customer, who would then go on to tell other people the good news.

The Data Centre was surprised at the number of people who responded and pleased at how many gave great feedback. Importantly, they also learnt a few new things about their customers and the service they provided and were able to tweak their branding messages and marketing strategies accordingly.

DON'T PROCRASTINATE; GET ON AND DO IT!

Although research into understanding your target market is certainly needed, don't overdo it. It's good to know what people are currently thinking and feeling but I have seen some companies who 'over-research' and end up with reams and reams of information that then becomes confusing. Sometimes they have a fantastic product but get so obsessed with the tiniest details that the idea never gets to market; or they love the creative ideas you have presented and 'can really see how it will push the brand to the next level' but, after sleeping on it, they get scared and decide to stick more-or-less with what they already have, which means they never progress as a brand. You can never know 100% whether an idea is going to work, but if you have a good gut feeling and believe in it, get the team behind it, then implement it thoroughly and with conviction. It can only go one of two ways...sometimes you just need to do it!

UNDERSTANDING WHAT TYPE OF BRAND YOU HAVE

To properly assess your target audience and make sure your branding fits perfectly, you need to make sure you're absolutely clear on what type of brand you have.

With your hierarchy in place, you should be able to quickly see the various brands in your portfolio. Next to each of these you can write a few short notes as to who that brand is aimed at and where those customers might come from. For example, the BMW X3 is a luxury brand, aimed at mums or mums-to-be with a certain household income, so a few places you might find those customers are:

- Via men who already own one of your cars and may be looking for their first family car (it's always easier to sell to existing customers)

- A female who already owns the BMW 1 series and has recently got married

- Mums' groups and 'Mumsnet' - you could suggest a joint promotion

- Facebook – perhaps run a photo competition, as women tend to enjoy posting pictures on their walls!

> **DON'T LET THE NOISE OF OTHERS' OPINIONS DROWN OUT YOUR OWN INNER VOICE...PEOPLE OFTEN THINK THEY WANT SOMETHING UNTIL THEY GET SHOWN AN ALTERNATIVE THEY NEVER THOUGHT POSSIBLE.**
>
> STEVE JOBS

Decide where your brand falls on the affordability scale – is it luxury, mid-range, budget or FMCG (Fast Moving Consumer Goods)? Mars and Green & Blacks are both chocolate brands, but target two very different audiences. The consumer instantly knows who the brand is targeting by the look and feel of the packaging design, which (though the consumer may be unaware) would have been through a long audience research and design process in order to ensure it captures the attention of the intended customer.

MARS

- Good, strong brand
- Mid-range priced product
- Font is fun and relaxed
- Mid-range packaging materials
- A more masculine feel has been created by using a simple bold font and bold colours.

GREEN & BLACKS

- Good, strong brand
- 'Created without compromise'
- High-end product
- Simple yet beautiful, 'classy' packaging
- A more female 'high-end' look has been created by using an elegant font and sophisticated colour palette.

Who your audience is and what type of brand you have will play a huge part in determining both the design of materials to communicate your brand and how you use those materials.

FOCUS GROUPS

Some organisations rely heavily on focus groups to gain so-called 'customer insight'. Personally, I don't think asking a group of strangers what they think of a particular colour, logo, name or tagline adds anything useful to the decision-making process for a brand's key elements. You usually end up spending lots of time and money and get a very varied response from people who don't really understand the brand's values.

In my opinion, it's much more worthwhile and cost-effective to informally discuss core decisions with a handful of internal and external people who you know understand the brand. They're usually pleased and flattered that you value their opinion and are likely to come up with honest, considered points that can be usefully debated. Always try and involve a diverse range of people; it's often the most unlikely ones that come up with the best ideas.

That being said, on some more general matters, focus groups can work very well. I worked with a certain beauty brand that wanted to be very transparent with its customers and list every ingredient contained in each beauty product next to it on the website. I argued that the majority of women didn't care about the specific ingredients; most probably wouldn't know either what a 'paraben' was or that it was in the majority of products currently on the market. I also explained that people don't read reams of copy on a website, especially an e-commerce site, where they simply want to know the key information and will click a 'read more' button if they want to understand in more detail.

Three small focus groups were arranged; the first two contained women of different ages who already had some kind of association with us or the client (this made them feel more relaxed) and the third contained beauty experts, who also had some kind of connection.

The results were very interesting. The consumers said they never read what was in a product because they thought that if they did, they might be put off! The majority hadn't heard of parabens and generally bought a product based on advertising, recommendation or from a brand they already trusted. They were happy to experiment and try different toiletry products, such as moisturising cream and shampoo, but when it came to cosmetics they tended to stick with the trusted brands they'd used for years.

The beauty experts were completely different because they were looking at it from a commercial viewpoint: does the product do what it claims it can do and does it come in suitable sizes for trade? And, yes, they would need to know what it did and didn't contain so they could use these facts to help sell the products to their clients. They also knew what a paraben was and felt it was important.

The results from the focus group allowed the client to understand their different audiences better. They could see what consumers and beauty professionals really wanted and that some of the things the client had thought were important were, in fact, not. As a result, they amended the website so that it had shorter copy next to each product and then more information on other pages, where the beauticians could find the details that would help them sell more effectively to their clients.

HOW TO COMPILE A FOCUS GROUP

To try something on the same scale as the beauty client we worked with, I would recommend the following:

- Decide what you want to find out and compile a suitable list of questions. They need to be structured in such a way that they require more than a 'yes' or 'no' answer.

- Compile a list of the people you'd like to speak to and decide if you need to split these into two or three groups, like we did with the 'general customer' and 'beauty expert'

- Choose a good mediator for the group/s - one who isn't going to influence their answers and will ensure everyone gets an equal say

- Have two people taking notes or video the session to make sure nothing's missed

- Hold the session somewhere quiet and relaxing, as you tend to get more out of people this way

CUSTOMER INSIGHT SESSION

If you want to gain a deeper insight into what your current customers want and think of your brand then it's a good idea to use a third party to carry out the research. If you approach an expert in this field, you'll find that they'll ask questions you would never have thought of asking – and some questions that it would be awkward for you to ask. They can also analyse the results and give you concise, constructive feedback.

HOW THIS ALL HELPS DEFINE THE MIXTURE REQUIRED TO CREATE THE 'TOTAL BRAND EXPERIENCE'

Understanding your brand's hierarchy, morals, values, and direction; getting the whole team involved; understanding your customers and then getting them on board, can all be combined to create an unstoppable brand.

You can throw thousands of pounds at advertising but if you're not part of your customers' lifestyle and culture, why would they bother with you?

I've worked on many projects over the years that have involved creating a 'Total Brand Experience' and understanding these key things has enabled us, as teams, to make great decisions on which ideas, elements and platforms to keep and which to ditch.

CASE STUDY: ZEPTER / TUTTOLUXO

When I was first appointed to work with Zepter UK, a company that sells high-end Swiss and Italian products globally, there was no plan in place regarding customer interaction and using multiple channels to grow the brand. At the time, their products were being sold through just a handful of sales consultants and, although the brand was extremely well-known in Europe, it was not known in the UK. Neither the logo, the website nor the other marketing collateral really encapsulated the essence of the brand, and there was no social media activity to be seen.

Part of the plan was to engage with more high-profile consumers for Zepter's skincare and cosmetics sub-brand, Tuttoluxo. As the product was mainly sold online with only a few actual salespeople, we needed to put something in place that would allow customers to experience the brand.

THE TUTTOLUXO TOTAL BRAND EXPERIENCE PLAN

I would lead the team in creating a new brand identity, stationery and other marketing materials. Year 1 would focus on increasing brand awareness with the end consumer and would consist of:

- Creating a stand-alone, e-commerce website for Tuttoluxo, which would include videos demonstrating the product (also on YouTube)

- Twitter and Facebook campaigns that integrated with other media, such as radio, email and their website

- Email campaigns to existing and potential customers

- Replacing the cheaper plastic bags with better quality ones, to be used at events

- Trialling products in beauty salons

- Forging affiliations to allow cross-promotion

- Attending a series of high-profile events where the product could be demonstrated

- Creating joint ventures with other suitable brands

Following feedback from both male and female focus groups that they would prefer to try a product before they bought it, we teamed up with the Swiss Tourism board and compiled a cross-promotion campaign in selected fitness centres around London.

I wanted to get more high-end consumers interacting with the brand and suggested a good way to raise Tuttoluxo's profile would be to feature at some of the lifestyle events that our target audience attended. After some research we selected:

Ladies' Day at Newbury. VIP goody bags were handed out by branded promotional girls and we ran radio, email and social media campaigns before, during and after the event.

Cartier International Polo. We had a branded marquee where promotional staff and beauticians gave away free hand and beauty massages all day, and a joint venture with one of the hospitality companies ensured we had a goody bag on every table in the VIP enclosure. We also promoted competitions before the event, via social media, email and the Tuttoluxo website, then used the same platforms to announce the competition winners and display photographs after the event.

Sandbanks Polo. This was the same format as for the Cartier Polo, except this time we had access to the players - quite a coup! We managed to get Jack Kidd (Jodie Kidd's brother and the England Team Captain) in for a massage, which was great for PR.

After the first year of executing the new Total Brand Experience plan, **Tuttoluxo and Zepter Cookware UK sales rose by 361%** (during a global recession). This generated subsequent consistent growth, with sales rising by another 23% the following year.

> **BEING PART OF YOUR CUSTOMERS' WORLD IS GOOD FOR BUSINESS. HELP PEOPLE WANT TO BUY FROM YOUR STORY.**
>
> SAM WILSON, WOLFF OLINS

AND ONE LAST POINT THAT IS OFTEN OVERLOOKED...

A TOTAL BRAND NEEDS THE RIGHT TONE OF VOICE

It's all very well interacting with your audience, but you must make sure you're using the right tone of voice in your marketing communications. That's the right tone of voice for your brand and the right tone of voice for your audience. There's no point using slang or text language when you're 'speaking' to corporate, high-end clients or the more serious media; similarly, a very corporate writing style won't suit 'chatty' consumer websites or necessarily appeal to a broad audience. A brand needs to be able to communicate on all levels and one thing I have learnt is that it's vital you get the right copywriter for the job. Each will have different skills, so make sure your team includes one or two copywriters that you know can communicate your message effectively, across all platforms.

IS THERE A BLUEPRINT TO BUILDING THE PERFECT BRAND?

I know there is. That's why I produced the 'brand blueprint', a step-by-step guide demonstrating how to build a more recognisable and successful brand.

It's full of creative ways to help you build the strong and lasting foundations that will enable you to establish and grow your brand successfully. Work through the exercises and you'll develop a clearer understanding of your brand foundations, and then use that information to accurately explain to a design agency what you want your brand to look and sound like. It's an effective starting point from which they can then put together and deliver effective designs and campaigns.

TO GET YOUR HANDS ON THE BLUEPRINT FOR BRAND SUCCESS

To get your hands on the FREE blueprint for brand success, please visit www.beyond-the-logo.com

WHY IS THIS LOGO 'THING' SO IMPORTANT?

THE LOGO, SYMBOL OR ICON YOU USE TO REPRESENT YOUR BRAND SHOULD REFLECT YOUR VISION AND POSITION. IT'S NOT JUST A 'THING' YOU STICK ON YOUR BUSINESS CARD; IT'S WHAT CREATES A GOOD OR BAD FIRST IMPRESSION AND IT TELLS YOUR AUDIENCE WHO YOU ARE.

YOUR LOGO WILL ENCOMPASS EVERYTHING YOUR BRAND IS AND WANTS TO BE. IT WILL REPRESENT THE BEATING HEART OF YOUR ORGANISATION AND YOU NEED TO LOVE AND CHERISH IT.

I'd like to start with a great example of how choosing the right logo can improve the performance of the whole company.

I was approached by BankToTheFuture (BF), a new business that needed help with its branding and website. The founders had already created a number of logos that had been used at various stages throughout the process of finalising the brand, which meant there were several versions floating around on different websites and they were still not happy with what they'd produced! Setting up a new business can be quite costly, so it's very common for founders to try and 'knock something up' themselves, thinking they can save money, but nearly all of them eventually realise it's a false economy. BF finally accepted this was something they simply couldn't do in-house.

We had a long discussion and I could see what they were trying to create, but what they had come up with so far just didn't portray their vision. Their criteria for the brand were:

- Friendly and clean

- DIDN'T look anything like a bank

- Something that would work well on various media, especially the website as this was the main driver for the business

They liked the Virgin brand and what it stood for, and also the cinema VUE, as their logo was always changing colour, giving it a continuous 'new look'. In terms of their target market, there were two: the 'Investor' and the 'Entrepreneur'. They felt the Investor was more likely to be very business-minded and the Entrepreneur a little more light-hearted.

I suggested the brand could have two colours, one for each audience, and a shorter version for online use. The end result really captured the essence of the brand:

BF

BANKTO THE**FUTURE**.COM®

Top:
Abreviated logo for online use.

Below:
Full logo with blue to represent
the 'investor' and purple for
the 'Entrepreneur'.

"Just before we launched BankToTheFuture.com, we decided to meet with Emma to check that we were on the right track with our brand. We were close to launch, but we just didn't feel as though our brand matched what we were up to in the world.

After spending a bit of time with Emma, we realised that we were way off. Emma got down to the core of what message we were trying to build into our business and why our existing brand did not make our team feel as proud as it could be.

After going through all the concepts Emma designed for us, we found the branding that represented exactly what we were about.

We rebranded every aspect of the business and a new energy took over the company. I never would have thought that redesigning and rebranding could make such a difference to our bottom line and performance, but it did!"

Simon Dixon, CEO & Co-Founder, BankToTheFuture.com

1898

1885

1905

1906

1940

1950

1962

1973

1991

1998

2005

2008

2008

Some brands stand the test of time and always look classic, whereas others find it hard to position themselves. If you take the time at the beginning to get it right, you can make your brand much stronger. Just look at how two very well-known rival brands compare in terms of how their branding has changed (or not) over the years (facing page).

It's interesting to see how Pepsi was trying to be similar to the already-established Coca-Cola at the beginning - maybe this 'copycat' approach is why they've always been seen as the underdog. The rebranding process must have been very costly to Pepsi over the years, given that every time the logo changes, everything has to change right across the organisation, from internal documents to advertising and packaging, right across the globe. Getting it right at the beginning makes it far easier and cheaper in the long run, especially when you're working across multiple platforms.

CREATING A NEW BRAND

This is pretty much a step into the unknown, which can be both exciting and daunting, and will either fail or succeed – and you won't know which until it's out there. That's why you need to research, plan, be committed, and then just have the nerve to go for it!

A new brand starts with nothing but your vision and business plan. You usually have no staff or possibly just one or two people who are there to help you launch the new brand. You need to understand your market, as your brand will need to appeal to and attract them, but, with no sales history, both you and the brand are going to need to work hard.

I was at a business networking event recently and spoke to a gentleman about branding. His opinion was: 'If you have a huge investor on board, why care about what the brand looks like? Surely you just need the money.' Well...money isn't everything - you can throw thousands at advertising but if your message and brand do not capture the attention of your audience and portray your values, it's game over! As I said in the previous chapter, today's audience is much more demanding and savvy and you need to have good foundations, so don't for one minute fall into the trap of thinking that money can make up for a logo and branding that's not quite right.

- Your company's core values and objectives

- The product or service itself

- Your target audience

- The platforms you might use

...then find a designer who understands where you want to go and can offer you a number of solutions.

Digital communications company, Orange, and the telephone banking brand, First Direct, are great examples of companies that have launched new brands very successfully, so take a look at them and how their branding represents their organisation and targets their audience.

WHY SOME COMPANIES REBRAND

With consumers and the world changing at the pace they have been for many years, it makes it hard for companies to keep up, but you need to keep up to stay in the game. This, along with other factors, such as mergers and acquisitions, means brands sometimes need refreshing.

Of course, refreshing a brand – especially if it's a large global organisation - is very time-consuming and expensive, but if it's going to grow market share or even just keep you in the game, it's worth every penny. For small and medium-sized businesses, such as Tuttoluxo in the example I used earlier, where the rebrand was only for the UK, it's a lot easier.

I believe you should take a step back from your brand every once in a while and ask yourself the following:

- Does our brand still say who we are?

- Do we need to up our game against our competitors?

- Are there other spaces we want to own and will our current brand allow us to do that?

THINGS TO CONSIDER...

- A logo isn't just a 'thing' that gets placed on random objects; it's the spokesperson for your business

- A strong visual identity builds trust and is essential to establishing and maintaining a presence in the marketplace

- Think of your logo as your best salesperson

- Whether a new brand or a re-brand:
  - What message are you trying to convey?
  - Who is your audience?
  - What colours are going to work and not work?
  - What font works best with your brand, in printed literature and on the web? (There are thousands of fonts to choose from and each encompasses a different 'feeling'.)
  - Do you need a shorter version of the logo (or symbol) that can be used for social media or if you're combining the brand with another, etc.?
  - Are there sub-brands to consider?

CREATING YOUR IDENTITY: THE DESIGN PROCESS

Every agency has their own way of working and some branding projects require a lot more stages than others, but here is a general guide to the process:

- The agency you've chosen will spend some time getting to know your brand and discussing your own ideas - what you are trying to say, etc. (If they have been helping you with your brand architecture, they'll already know this.)

- Competitors and brands whose profile and success you'd like to emulate will be researched

- The agency will then work on various concepts and decide which to present to you. Usually these will initially be in black and white so that you're not influenced by any particular colour.

- There is generally some further experimentation with the one or two options you've chosen

- Different colours are then added, to see how the logo will work on different types of media and material

- The final logos are created as vector files, which allows you to enlarge them as much as you like, without pixilation. (Any designer who tries to sell them to you in other formats, such as Word, Paintshop Pro or Photoshop, is not doing their job properly and should be dismissed!)

Before approaching an agency, make sure you understand why you're approaching them and go armed with plenty of information about your brand and what you want. Ask them about their process (i.e. how they work with clients) so you have a clear understanding from the outset. Good communication makes projects run a lot more smoothly!

It's important to make sure you choose the right agency - one that really understands what you want to achieve – and, personally, I don't believe a design agency needs to have experience in the same industry or sector as yours. A good designer will be able to adapt and relate to multiple industries and you quite often find that someone from outside your industry will create something really original and inspiring, as they're looking at it with fresh eyes. When I was pitching for the branding work with BlueSquare Data, we were up against another agency that had already worked with other data centres. But because I hadn't worked in that particular field before, I created something that was quite different to the branding of all their competitors and we won the pitch.

WHAT'S THE POINT IN HAVING THE SAME KIND OF LOGO AS YOUR COMPETITOR? DON'T ALWAYS PLAY SAFE, BE BRAVE WITH YOUR BRAND AND AMAZING THINGS COULD HAPPEN...

EXERCISE:

I'd like you to read through the below
and imagine you are the person in the scenario.

1. THE SCENARIO...

- You've been in a high managerial position for 10yrs +
- You've just been made redundant
  and have been given a good payout
- You're not ready to retire
- You fancy being your own boss but don't want
  the stress of setting up a business from scratch

2. YOUR WISH LIST...

- To be your own boss
- To manage a team without doing the dirty work
- Something that isn't another start-up business
- To have fun, enjoy life and earn enough money
  to be able to spend time doing the things you like

3. YOUR DECISION...

To find a franchise that allows you
to do everything on your wish list.

4. YOU ATTEND A FRANCHISE SHOW...

The first two franchises you come across are A and B.
Which one looks like it most matches your wish list?

A.

You might be thinking...

- you will have to do all the work
- it's a little cheap-looking
- it's not the serious, high-end brand you're looking for
- it won't give you either the return on investment or the lifestyle you are after

B.

You may think:

- it can give you the lifestyle you want
- the earnings look more in line with what you require
- it looks more professional and high-end than Franchise A

The comments on A and B were some of the comments I received when presenting this scenario to 30 people. In reality, with both:

- You can achieve a turnover of £500,000 in 4 years
- You will be managing a large team and possibly employing up to 100 people
- There is a huge market potential

You'll probably now not be surprised to find out that A and B are, in fact, the same brand.

The difference is that version A was created by an agency that didn't fully understand the brand or its target market, whereas version B was created by an agency that did.

Alan, the founder of the Adept Cleaning franchise, actually had a very clear idea who the business was aimed at and where they were in the marketplace. Unfortunately, the design agency that he initially chose to work with didn't understand either how important a consideration this was or that there were two target audiences: prospective franchisees and the end consumer. It also looks like they didn't even understand how the franchise business works, as the messaging certainly wasn't suitable for that audience.

Adept Cleaning wanted to attract franchisees that had the skills and experience to manage a large team, possibly with a corporate background. They would be the type of person who wanted to manage and grow a cleaning business, rather than actually scrub the floors themselves. We needed to ensure the brand stood out from other cleaning franchises and appealed to manager types who wanted a business that would allow them to live a high-end lifestyle.

To achieve this, we used aspirational lifestyle images to demonstrate the type of things people could end up doing if they joined Adept. We then overhauled the old literature (which failed to highlight the main selling point: the potential earnings) and used the existing orange corporate colour to highlight the most important information and key benefits throughout the brochure, while maintaining brand consistency. This also meant potential franchisees could skim the literature and quickly and easily make a decision as to whether they wanted to have a further conversation.

To keep the message consistent, it was important that the paper also reflected the high-end feel, so a heavy, uncoated stock was used. Printed collateral is very tangible, so it's important that when people touch anything with your brand on, it conveys the right message.

(And I'd like to say a big thank you to Alan, the founder of Adept Cleaning, for allowing me to use his company in this example.)

REMEMBER

Remember this 'thing' that is your logo is going to be seen everywhere – on your stationery, in social media, on your website, in videos, at events and - much, much more. It's what is used to headline the presentation of your organisation to everybody, everywhere.

BRAND CONSISTENCY:
HOW TO MAKE A BRAND CONSISTENT AND WHY IT'S SO IMPORTANT

YOUR BRAND WILL BE PRESENTED ACROSS MULTIPLE PLATFORMS AND TO A MULTITUDE OF PEOPLE. THROUGH IT, YOU'RE TRYING TO BUILD A RELATIONSHIP NOT ONLY WITH CURRENT AND PROSPECTIVE CUSTOMERS, BUT ALSO INTERNAL STAFF, SUPPLIERS, AFFILIATES AND POTENTIAL BUSINESS PARTNERS, THEREFORE YOU HAVE TO BE CONSISTENT AND CLEAR IN EVERYTHING YOU DO.

A set of varying logos and messages confuses people and if you look like a confused brand people will assume the company is also run in a confused manner. When you're a small company, that's fairly easy to manage, but when you become larger it gets more complicated. Again, if you build the right foundations at the beginning, your brand is easier to control as you grow. Never assume you will always be small: the world is your oyster and anything is possible and achievable!

Working with small companies that have then gone on to grow much larger has allowed me to see first-hand not only how useful but also how important brand guidelines are:

1. They set the scene for 'who' the company is, its beliefs and values, etc.

2. They detail what you can and can't do with the logo, what an email campaign layout should look like, advert formats, how literature should look, etc.

3. They help new staff to understand the brand.

Guidelines clarify everything to do with the company's branding, and the process of compiling them actually helps create much better, stronger, more consistent brands.

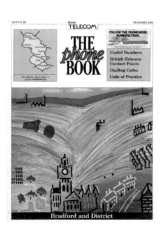

You may or may not remember, but in the early days of British Telecom (BT), the brand was very inconsistent, thanks to almost every county in the UK playing around with different designs for the cover of their famous telephone book. This turned the brand into something of a mess.

In contrast, BT now has a consistent brand that also regularly reinvents itself to stay ahead – a necessity in today's world, where telephone and broadband have become ever-more competitive and technology is moving at a great pace. The 'piper' logo (which came under great scrutiny when it was launched in 1991) was about

talking, and the 'Connected World' globe logo (launched in 2003) embraces multimedia communications. Brand guidelines will now be in place to ensure every part of BT communicates a consistent message.

Guidelines are particularly important for franchises, where there are multiple business owners operating under one brand. Franchisees often have very varied backgrounds; some understand branding and the importance of a consistent message and others don't. It's therefore essential that this is not only explained at the beginning, but that they also have a document they can refer to when they're creating their own communications. Businesses franchise in order to grow quickly in multiple locations, under one brand. If franchisees start messing around with corporate branding, you end up with what's supposed to be a coherent message and identity becoming diluted, the brand potentially being damaged because of a drop in branding quality and, in the worst cases, consumers not even realising it's the same company!

Over the years I've been approached by lots of franchisees who've wanted to change copy and images on documents and every time I've had to explain why it can't be done. I think the most extreme one was when I was approached by the franchisee of a well-known business coaching franchise who didn't like the look of the brand and wanted not only a new business card created but also a new logo. The whole point of buying into a franchise is because you trust and like the brand, not because you think there's something wrong with it!

WHAT SHOULD THE BRAND GUIDELINES DOCUMENT CONTAIN?

Brand guidelines will be used by a variety of internal staff and external suppliers, such as designers, PR agencies and manufacturers. They need to be easy to understand and contain all the important elements relevant to your business. They generally include the following:

- A brief introduction to the organisation/brand
- Mission – vision – values
- Logo sizing and spacing
- Colour, including Pantone references, etc.
- Typefaces

- Tone of voice
- Imagery and tone for imagery
- Stationery
- Literature principles
- PowerPoint or Keynote style
- Website and any other online applications
- Signage
- Office environments
- Any other key documents

Guidelines are there to protect the core brand and ensure it's not abused, such as the colour of the logo being changed. But they shouldn't be so strict that they stop creativity, and it's a good idea to review them every so often to make sure the brand stays relevant and doesn't become stale.

For example, a few years ago no one knew what a social media icon was, but now brands are adding them everywhere. How these are managed, where they should appear and the tone of voice that should be used in communicating through these new channels should be added to the guidelines, if appropriate. A brand needs to evolve with the changing market.

Having a clear brand identity makes it easier to communicate your brand across different channels. If you use social media, video, print, etc. and the brand looks different in each channel, the audience will be confused and it's a costly mistake to fix. Clarify your brand guidelines at the start and they'll enable you to ensure the brand stays clear and consistent as you move forward.

THE FINER DETAILS

HAVE YOU EVER SEEN A DESIGN YOU LIKE AND YOU'RE NOT SURE WHY YOU LIKE IT OR WHY IT WORKS, THERE'S JUST SOMETHING ABOUT IT? OR YOU TRY AND EXPLAIN TO A DESIGNER THAT YOU LIKE SUCH-AND-SUCH AND WHEN THEY ASK WHY, YOU CAN'T ANSWER THEM. MAYBE YOU'VE SEEN SOMETHING YOU LIKE AND TRIED TO RECREATE IT BUT IT JUST DOESN'T QUITE HAVE THE SAME FEELING...

WELL, THAT'S BECAUSE DESIGNING - WHETHER FOR THE WEB, PRINT OR EVENTS. - ISN'T SIMPLY A CASE OF THROWING SOME IMAGES ON A PAGE WITH A BIT OF COPY AND, HEY PRESTO, IT'S DONE. THERE ARE MANY, MANY ELEMENTS WE 'CREATIVES' CONSIDER WHEN DESIGNING SOMETHING TO CREATE THAT PERFECT BRAND EXPERIENCE - YOU'D BE AMAZED AT WHAT GOES ON IN A DESIGNER'S MIND!

BUT YOU DON'T NEED (OR NECESSARILY WANT) TO KNOW ALL ABOUT HOW MY HEAD WORKS, SO IN THIS CHAPTER I'M JUST GOING TO GIVE YOU A QUICK INSIGHT INTO SOME OF THE FINER POINTS.

TYPOGRAPHY

I could talk about typography all day; there are so many beautiful and functional fonts available. Each conveys a different tone and is suitable for different audiences and media, so think about what your font says about your organisation. This goes back to the foundations you built: take who you are, what it is you're selling and who you're selling it to and really look at whether the font you use is the most appropriate one.

Is your brand more suited to Neometric or Angelina? (And a side note: please don't EVER use Comic Sans; it's awful – you may already know designers hate it!) Take a look at the next page to see a few examples of fonts that tend to evoke quite strong feelings.

Taglines and sign-offs need to use a font that complements your logo - again this goes back to what message you're trying to convey and what image you want to portray.

IS THE COPY LEGIBLE AND READABLE?

In the design world, 'legibility' and 'readability' have particular meanings and relevance that might be outside what you immediately understand by the words.

Legibility is how easy it is to recognise bursts of copy, which is dictated by the contrast between the type and the background colour. A couple of examples:

- Black type on a white background gives the highest contrast (although, interestingly, this is not very suitable for dyslexics)

- White type on a black background may be striking, but it's not easy to read long blocks of copy and is certainly not good for the elderly.

gon

Meta Serif

BEE

k GOTHIC *angelina*

BLACKO

eva lintel

kabe

nissan

zu

Pl

helvetica neue

eda

Bodoni

STENCIL

M

snell roun

Gill Sans

rev

nuhaus

yonna

sa

Century Go

SEWOOD znikomit

AS

K

BICUBIK

neometri

trebuch

bradley hand

plakative grotesk

ch

Arual

NCETOWN

sweetly broker

Lyc

a Lisa

DIN

and courier

advent

e

Meta

impact

enigmatic

vezus

skia

ye

ic

tura

ECCENTRI

verda

Readability is making sure it's easy enough to read that the reader doesn't lose their flow/tracking. From a design point of view, this means keeping lines to a comfortable reading length (usually 8-10 words per line); not too long to scan easily and not so short that they interrupt the reading flow. That being said, creativity is creativity and you may want to design a more abstract title with the copy split onto shorter lines. Just be aware of the impact of the design on the readability of the piece. In terms of font sizes, generally speaking:

- 7-10pt is a comfortable size for reading, unless you are targeting the elderly, in which case you may want to increase it

- 10-14pt is more suitable for use on the web, although the browser's zoom tool can be used to increase the size

Some fonts have also been designed for specific use, such as large blocks of copy; for example, a book is more suited to certain serif or humanist sans serif fonts as these are more readable and legible. Others are more practical for short titles.

We designers are always looking to improve the quality and experience of our work, so will often try to enhance the legibility and readability of a client's branding and copy by increasing the 'leading' (the space between the lines) and the 'tracking' (space between the characters). These are functions you may not have access to on something like MS Word, which is why you might find that when you try to replicate a designer's work, it doesn't look quite the same!

WHY WOULD YOU NEED TO TEST A FONT FOR YOUR BRAND?

Selecting the correct font is usually fairly easy, but some projects do require testing. I worked with a company called Dancing Kites, which produces books specifically aimed at dyslexic children, therefore the tracking and font size is imperative to their success. We needed to not only check the readability but also the legibility and ideal page size.

Several options were tested with children of varying ages and different degrees of dyslexia. We also found a font that had been specifically designed for dyslexia sufferers but, unfortunately, it wasn't available to purchase, which was a tremendous shame. Nevertheless, I was very pleased with what we produced and Dancing Kites have had some great testimonials, including:

"The quality of the books is amazing – they are well written, beautifully illustrated and very professionally packaged."

Chris Hooton, Orchadis Media

"Fantastic books. I love the format: lovely bright pictures, not overwhelming, clear, interesting and stimulating."

T.Coxhead

Activate the Augmented Reality on the image above using the BeyondCT App.

LAYOUT AND COPY

I see far too many clients that want refreshing, expensive-looking designs that are easy to read, then give us pages and pages of copy to squeeze into a relatively tiny space.

Designs need 'white space' to allow the copy, images and message to breathe. You may have lots you want to communicate, but when it comes to making an impact on your audience, less is usually more. Just because you have a blank space doesn't mean you have to fill it!

The more white space you have, the more expensive and exclusive your brand will look and feel.

In terms of web design, users tend to scan rather than read, so keeping copy short with specific headlines will help the users find what they're looking for and keep them focused.

PAPER AND PRINTING TECHNIQUES

Going beyond just a logo and creating the Total Brand Experience certainly includes thinking about the type of paper you use. Although people say print is dead and digital is taking over, I believe companies will always require something that's printed. We just love to touch and feel, and something printed is so tangible. Combining print and digital media together in one campaign or on one physical item (I will explain more about this in the 'Direct Mail' section in Chapter 6) can result in something very playful and attractive to a wider audience.

With the advances in digital printing, it's now possible to get short runs of marketing materials printed, meaning you don't have to spend a lot of money in one go or hold stock that may be obsolete before you've had the chance to use it all.

Digital printing used to be very poor quality, but now it's almost as good as lithographic (litho). Because litho printing uses a lot more processes, the set-up costs are larger. This tends to make short runs expensive but larger runs

EXAMPLES:
These two examples show how an advert for a high-end brand can instantly lose its luxury appeal by having too much copy squeezed into one area.

Having too much information can stop the really important information from standing out. You only have a few seconds to grab a reader's attention so make sure your copy is concise and really hits the key benefits of what you're selling.

Printing processes:

Digital: The design is converted into a high-res pdf and then printed out on a digital printer, which basically looks like an industrial-sized photocopier.

Litho: The design is put onto printing plates - a different one for each colour - which are then inserted into the printer. Ink is added and the sheets of paper are then passed through the machine.

much cheaper per unit than digital printing. Conversely, digital has a higher cost per page than litho, which is why it's usually used for small runs but works out more expensive on a larger run.

The quality and colour you get from litho printing is superb, because it uses inks, meaning you can also use special inks, such as gold, silver or Pantone colours. But with any printing, make sure you always get samples from the printer, as there are certainly good and bad ones.

Customers, in my opinion, are likely to spend more with a brand if its brochure is printed on a heavy stock and the design has obviously been well-conceived, rather than if they have gone for the same type of paper used for pizza delivery flyers!

We, as consumers, want to positively experience a brand right from our first contact with it. This can be in the form of a memorable business card, a tactile brochure or how a company displays their products in beautifully-designed packaging...right down to how we feel when we unwrap the item at home.

Apple is a great example of a company that really understands the importance of refining the finer detail. The customer gets the brand experience from the moment they walk into a store right through to when they get home and open the packaging.

REMEMBER, FIRST IMPRESSIONS COUNT

If you're going to hand out a piece of printed material, make sure it sells your brand. I spend a lot of money on business cards. They're printed on extra-thick board, with silver or coloured foil either side, and die cut. Yes, they're expensive, but they're worth it, as the quality shines through and people usually make a point of talking about them.

Large corporates may see this as an unnecessary spend but, regardless of the size of your business, you still need great cards and brochures to sell your brand when interacting face to face. A brand has seconds to impress and handing over a badly-designed card on flimsy paper can undo a lot of the good work you've done so far. Show people you care about every aspect of your business and make your brand a talking point for the right reasons.

A PICTURE IS WORTH A THOUSAND WORDS.

FRED R. BARNARD

NATIONAL ADVERTISING MANAGER OF STREET RAILWAYS ADVERTISING IN THE 1920S

PHOTOGRAPHY

Good quality images that reflect your vision and mission will really help support your brand's message and attract your audience.

You can either seek the help of a professional to produce a selection of custom shots for your brand, go for stock photography, or use a mixture of the two. There are advantages and disadvantages to both:

STOCK PHOTOGRAPHY

Advantages: Can be cheap

Instantly available to download

Disadvantages: Nothing stops competitors using the same image, unless you buy the rights outright, which can be expensive

You can spend hours searching for just the right image

You may not be able to find exactly the right image and have to compromise

| Tips: | Always check the licence |
| | It's always a good idea to buy the high-res version, so it can be used on both digital and print campaigns |

HIRING A PROFESSIONAL

Advantages:	You usually own the images outright
	You control the shots and can get an ideal image
	It can sometimes work out cheaper than buying stock images if you can shoot several items in one day
Disadvantages:	Can be expensive for a 'one off' shot
	Can be time consuming
Tips:	Check how many shots the photographer will let you keep for a day's shoot
	Make a shooting list beforehand and discuss your requirements with the photographer, as special equipment may be needed
	Check whether you will own all the images outright, or whether you have to pay an annual licence fee

Although some of the things I've talked about may seem trivial, I promise you that they're all vital considerations if you want to come up with the best possible design solution. Whether it's printed materials, your website or a digital campaign, it's the finer details that will really enhance the way you communicate with your audience and help make your brand what it aspires to be.

NOW THAT YOU HAVE YOUR BRAND ARCHITECTURE IN PLACE, YOU KNOW YOUR AUDIENCE, YOU'VE MADE SURE YOUR BRAND IS CONSISTENT AND HAVE THOUGHT ABOUT THE FINER DETAILS, IT'S TIME TO LOOK AT THE VARIOUS COMMUNICATION PLATFORMS OR CHANNELS AVAILABLE TO YOUR BRAND. YOU CAN THEN DECIDE WHICH ONES YOU WANT TO MIX TOGETHER TO CREATE YOUR UNIQUE TOTAL BRAND EXPERIENCE.

IN THIS NEXT SECTION, YOU'LL ALSO SEE HOW INCORPORATING THE RIGHT TYPOGRAPHY, PAPER AND PHOTOGRAPHY INTO THE ITEMS IN THE FOLLOWING CHAPTERS WILL ENHANCE AND REINFORCE THE EXPERIENCE PEOPLE HAVE WHEN THEY COME INTO CONTACT WITH YOUR BRAND.

THE BRAND JOURNEY

Here is a Brand Map I have designed to explain the journey you need to take in order to create your brand and the 'Total Brand Experience'.

The 'stations' between 'Your Brand' and 'Your Logo' will help you understand and build your brand foundations. These will not only help you develop a strong brand, but will ensure the look of any piece of design is in tune with your audience and conveys your brand's core message.

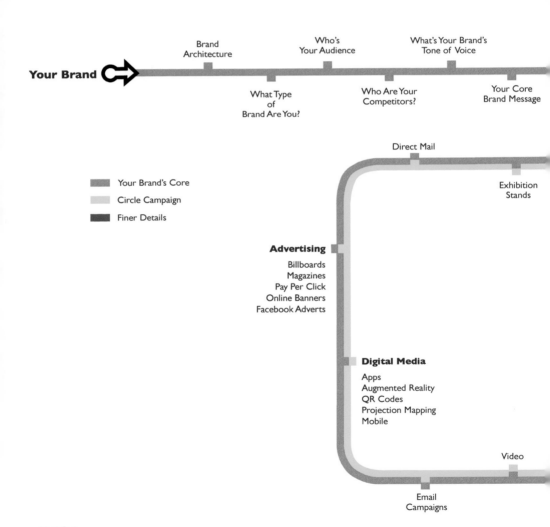

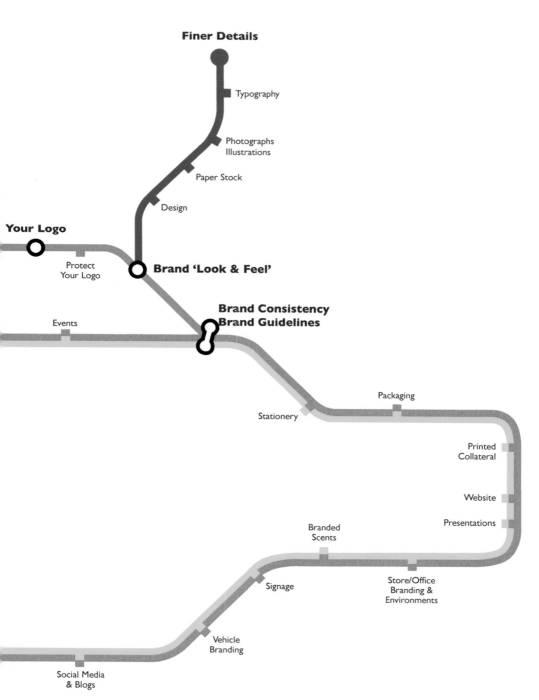

Finer Details

Typography

Photographs
Illustrations

Paper Stock

Design

Your Logo

Protect
Your Logo

Brand 'Look & Feel'

Brand Consistency
Brand Guidelines

Events

Packaging

Stationery

Printed
Collateral

Website

Presentations

Branded
Scents

Store/Office
Branding &
Environments

Signage

Vehicle
Branding

Social Media
& Blogs

SECTION TWO:
PROMOTING YOUR BRAND

DIRECT MAIL ISN'T DEAD, IT'S JUST GROWN UP!

BEFORE EMAIL AND SOCIAL MEDIA, 'SNAIL MAIL' WAS ONE OF THE MAIN MEDIA BUSINESSES WOULD USE TO COMMUNICATE WITH EXISTING AND NEW CUSTOMERS. OVER TIME, IT GOT A BAD REPUTATION FOR BEING 'JUNK MAIL' SO, WHEN IT BECAME POSSIBLE TO SEND EMAIL AND TEXT MESSAGE CAMPAIGNS, HUGE NUMBERS OF BUSINESSES MOVED OVER TO TRY THE 'NEW FAD'.

BUT DIRECT MAIL (SNAIL MAIL) HAS COME ON A LONG WAY AND, WITH THE ADVANCES IN TECHNOLOGY AND MORE COMPLEX MAILING LISTS, IT'S NOW SERIOUSLY GROWN UP!

SO, WHAT'S CHANGED?

In the early days of direct mail, the information on your mailing list for prospects and existing customers was pretty impersonal. The mailshot item would usually be a fairly generic letter, addressed to: Name, Surname, Position, and the lists would simply be categorised by household income and profile A, B or C, etc.

In today's world we can do a multitude of things to make the item you're sending far more interesting, relevant and personal to the recipient than was possible before.

With the advances in print technology - and particularly the vast improvement in the quality of digital printing - variations within one direct mail campaign can be printed all in one run. A good example of this is a dog charity that wanted to ask everyone on its mailing list for a donation. Its database contained details of what breed of dog each person had and, when the campaign was printed, not only did every mailing have the recipient's name inside, it also had an image of the particular breed of dog they owned. Making it personal in this way substantially increased the response rate.

An Infotrends/Cap Ventures study, The Value of Colour, found that personalised colour printing increased:

- Response rates by 36%
- Response time by 33.9%
- Average order size/value by 24.5%
- Orders/order retention by 47.6%
- Overall revenue/profit by 31.6%

Another example is Fitness First, which wanted to encourage more people to join their gyms. They also wanted to show customers that their nearest gym was only a short distance away. In their campaign, the back of each item featured a personalised map, showing the house where the recipient lived and where their nearest gym was.

Although compiling this kind of data might take time, the print process is relatively easy, as the printer automatically reads and interprets the data as it goes along.

This kind of technology means campaigns can be smaller and more targeted, giving better results for businesses, while still remaining affordable. It also means you can run smaller pilot/test campaigns before committing your entire budget.

INTEGRATE FOR 'THE TOTAL BRAND EXPERIENCE'

The basic aim of direct mail is to generate a response from the person to whom you are sending it and that's the same with any campaign, whether you're using printed or digital media.

As I've mentioned before, customers today not only want to communicate with brands, but are also more demanding and complex in the way they shop. A brand today needs to communicate on more than one platform to achieve the total experience, therefore direct mail should not be seen as one stand-alone dimension; it should integrate.

Integration isn't just a case of sticking your web address on the bottom of a piece of direct mail; it can involve adding videos, QR codes, or even augmented reality (see Chapter 8). No one customer is the same as another, so some will respond better to a printed campaign than an email and vice versa. And with email campaigns now having also been tarnished with the

Martin,

Let's start your journey...

Your nearest club is Glasgow and is only [...] miles away. It will take you less than 3 mi[...] to cycle to the gym - a perfect warm up!

Use the personalised map to help find us [...] we'll guide you on a journey to improve y[...] health, fitness and change the way you fe[...] about yourself.

Pop into the club today or call the number [...] below.

Looking forward to seeing you in the club [...]

Call and make the world a fitter pl[...]

0844 571 28 6[...]

or visit www.fitnessfirst.co.uk for more inform[...]

Never has getting in shape been so rewarding!

Fitness First's very own **FIRST CLUB** offers our members FREE access to exclusive offers, discounts and rewards on great products from brands you recognise - it's our way of saying thanks.

YOUR MEMBER[...] CAN PAY FOR ITS[...]

WE CAN HELP YOU
ACHIEVE YOUR
GOALS

FREE
1-DAY GUEST
MEMBERSHIP*
For you and a friend

Call in today and make the world a **fitter** place

fitnessFirs[...]

same 'junk mail' brush as direct mail, and ever-more sophisticated spam filters on the market, combining a print and digital campaign is definitely a better way of communicating with your audience and will ensure you capture a greater number of responses.

The insurance company More Th>n has now started to combine email and direct mail campaigns, after years of having had each type of distribution handled by different departments. It amazes me that in a world that is so integrated, so many companies still keep things segmented in this way. Businesses need to spend more time looking at how to integrate multiple platforms in a way that works best for them.

'For many companies, it's still early days for the integration of print and email. Too often, the decision to run an email campaign is based on whether a company has an email address, rather than what is the most appropriate channel.'

Scott Logie, Strategy Director of direct marketing provider, Occam

WHAT ELSE HAS CHANGED?

It's not just technology that's changed; it's also the types of people companies are now targeting. Direct mail is still more expensive than a quick email blast (unless you're integrating a video as part of the campaign), so sending out a beautifully-designed mailing to everyone you happen to have an address for is not cost effective! Overall, the top 100 companies that use direct mail - which includes Direct Wines, Boots and Saga - now invest more in mailings to existing customers than they do to prospects, as digital is becoming the channel of choice for this. Virgin Media, however, still use direct mail for both customer retention and prospecting for new business.

It all depends on your target market as to which approach will work best and you may have to experiment to find the right route for your brand and budget. It's always easier to sell to existing customers than to find new ones, so investing a little more in how you communicate with your current customers will make all the difference. You need to show the people you do business with that they're important to you and that you care about their loyalty, so don't simply send a 'blanket' email campaign. Think about how you could create a video email that's personalised for each customer or a nicely-designed and printed direct mail.

The easiest and most cost-effective way to dispatch a direct mail campaign is via a professional fulfilment company. Many times, I've seen small companies try to save money by purchasing stamps for a direct mail campaign themselves and getting internal staff to compile and post the items. Although they think they're saving money, once you've calculated the time spent putting the item together – that's time NOT spent on running the rest of the business - plus the fact that they've had to buy the stamps at full retail price, it's actually a false economy. As well as getting the job done efficiently, a fulfilment company can also buy the stamps at a better rate.

> ## NOT EVERYBODY WANTS TO 'GO DIGITAL'; THE CONSUMER'S JOURNEY IS NOT LINEAR ANYMORE – THERE ARE MULTIPLE TOUCH POINTS.
>
> PETE MARKEY, CHIEF MARKETING OFFICER AT MORE TH>N'S PARENT COMPANY, RSA INSURANCE GROUP, MARKETING MAGAZINE, 26 OCT 2011

With more brands switching focus to existing customers, Richard Marshal, Managing Partner at communications agency TMW, says, "This leaves more budget for creative direct mail. There's still nothing more impactful than a well-crafted, well-targeted mail pack". TMW created a direct mail campaign for financial services provider First Direct, with two versions of a 'pass the parcel' party game pack. The first was an 'award pack', which targeted 1,000 current customers and delivered a member-get-member message between several layers of newspaper. A harmonica was included as a prize, along with a £50 iTunes voucher that was redeemable for every friend who opened an account. The second pack, which went to 20,000 customers, still used the member-get-member mechanic but in a slightly less creative format.

The results indicated that a high percentage of those contacted would recommend First Direct to a friend. One customer took this a little further and phoned in to say that it was the most original thing he'd received in a long time, completely unexpected from a bank, and that he would be recommending First Direct to everybody. He signed off by playing a tune on his mouth organ!

WHAT PEOPLE REALLY THINK...

I conducted a bit of research to find out what people really think of direct mail and to see if the stigma of 'junk mail' still exists. Here are a few of the responses from marketers, business strategists and entrepreneurs:

"Direct mail certainly isn't dead, far from it. The advantages direct mail has over every other form of advertising is most of your competition won't know what you're up to. With knowledge of certain software tools on the internet, your competition can put you out of business fast. Not so with direct mail."

Clive Cable, Master Copywriter | B2B Lead Generation and Conversion

"Direct mail seems, on the face of it, to be much more expensive than email. But many people's inboxes are so stuffed full that it's hard to cut through with an email and, unless you have their 'double opt in' permission to send the email, it's likely to be rejected. Social media marketing is very fashionable but it is easy to be intrusive in an inappropriate way in this channel. Given that direct mail is expensive, it has to be very carefully designed to create impact and targeted to be relevant, but it can have great impact. Some of the most experienced direct marketers (e.g. Daryton Bird) still use direct 'snail' mail, so I guess it all depends how well you do it (like most things!)."

Chris Radford, Strategy Consultant and entrepreneur

"Direct mail is an effective tool when it's used well. The information needs to be emotive, otherwise the words won't even get read. Words only paint pictures, which then drive emotions, and this is where the real message is held. The more emotive a piece of communication is, the more likely it will be to hold people's attention."

Simon Clarkson, Director, Think Works

"Email responses and click-throughs are declining rapidly. To stand out now, a piece of creative, well-targeted direct mail is what cuts through."

Steve Stretton, Founding Partner of agency, Archibald Ingall Stretton.

HOW TO CREATE A GOOD DIRECT MAIL CAMPAIGN

Your campaign needs to grab the attention of the recipient the moment they first see it. The basic principles behind a good, strong campaign are to have a clear idea of who you're targeting and what you want to say. And make sure the design agency you are using understands direct mail, because some agencies specialise in different areas. Speak to the designer as early as possible in the process, as they will be able to suggest some more creative ideas, both in terms of options for the design of the campaign and how your database could be used.

If the design agency you're working with doesn't have a copywriter, I thoroughly recommend finding a good one to work with - or making sure someone in your in-house marketing team has the appropriate skills.

When I get a brief from a client – for example, 'we want a double-sided A5 postcard to advertise XYZ, with such-and-such on the front and back' - I usually consider their basic idea and then look at other options that will push the boundaries and result in a better response. I present them with three versions: their original idea, one concept that takes them to the next level without being too extreme and then another that pushes them to think differently.

I pitched a series of ideas to AHF, a furniture retail store similar to Furniture Village, and part of the pitch was to create ideas for their direct mail campaign, which they stated had to be in the form of a C5 postcard.

The campaign was going to run at Christmas and needed to appeal not only to current customers but also to a new, younger audience that the company wanted to attract.

Idea 1: This was a 'safe' campaign, split between existing customers and prospects. The existing customer would get invited to a 'Members Only' evening with extra discounts. The prospects would simply receive a postcard advertising the sale. I created a more stylish look than they had previously used for their campaigns, as I felt this would appeal more to their target market.

Idea 2: Research has shown that people respond better to pictures of the opposite sex and that personalised colour printing increases response rates by 36%. With the data the company already held, we could personalise the campaign by using different pictures and copy for each sex and could also take this a step further by having different images not only for each sex but also for different age brackets.

AHF were impressed with how we could use their existing database to make the campaign more targeted, and they liked the cheeky element we had added to each design. This was a little bit of small print which said, 'Unfortunately, the man/woman is not included in the sale, but we do sell equally sexy furniture...'

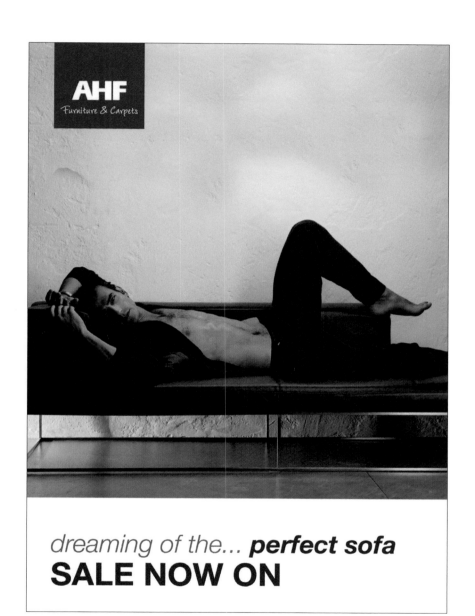

*dreaming of the... **perfect sofa***
SALE NOW ON

Idea 3: This campaign was clearly split for the two different target audiences: the current customer, who tended to be slightly older, and the younger audience they wanted to attract into the store. The campaign's aim was to show the variety of items sold in-store by using something a little different to a postcard and playing on the Christmas theme.

AHF loved the quirky design and how we had taken what was meant to be a postcard and turned it on its head into something more eye-catching and unusual. They also liked how we had managed to create a design that would not only appeal to existing customers but could be adapted to attract the younger audience they were hoping for.

DECK THE HALLS

(AND THE LIVING ROOM AND THE DINING ROOM AND THE BEDROOM...)

Another example is a direct mail campaign I designed as part of a larger project with BlueSquare Data, who wanted to invite a small number of prospects and customers to attend the official opening of their new data centre. The mailing contained details of the event, including: key speakers, such as Ben Cohen from Channel 4; information on the new data centre with a small map; a stamped addressed R.S.V.P. for those who wanted to post a response and an email address for those who wanted to email. The invitation was also sent as an email campaign.

Direct mail certainly isn't dead, and many customers I speak to about how it has changed are surprised at how sophisticated it's become. By combining new technology (like augmented reality and variable data), direct mail, great copy and creative design, you can create a really powerful and effective campaign.

KNOCKING UP A QUICK WEBSITE

I'M OFTEN ASKED IF I CAN 'JUST KNOCK UP A QUICK WEBSITE'. I THINK THIS IS BECAUSE BUSINESSES KNOW THEY NEED ONE BUT ARE NOT SURE WHY! THEY DON'T UNDERSTAND THE VALUE THAT TAKING THE TIME TO CREATE A GOOD WEBSITE CAN ADD TO THEIR BUSINESS, OR RECOGNISE THE EXPERTISE PROFESSIONALS CAN ADD. SOMETIMES, THEY SIMPLY BELIEVE THE MONEY WOULD BE BETTER SPENT ELSEWHERE IN THE BUSINESS.

IF YOU WANT A 'QUICK' WEBSITE, YOU CAN JUST BUY A TEMPLATE AND DO IT YOURSELF, BUT IT WILL NEVER BE AS EFFECTIVE AS A PROFESSIONAL, BESPOKE WEBSITE. THIS CHAPTER DETAILS WHY, AND EXPLAINS THE PROCESS OF DESIGNING AND CREATING SOMETHING THAT WILL GIVE YOUR BUSINESS AN ONLINE PRESENCE THAT NOT ONLY REPRESENTS BUT ALSO ENHANCES YOUR BRAND.

When I first started working in web design, sites were built in a completely different way, broadband was unheard of for home use and there was no such thing as Facebook!

Today, we have some great technology. One big leap in development is that we no longer have to use Flash to add a simple bit of animation to a website. We can now also integrate videos, blogs and social media, which add to the user's experience and allow us to communicate on a completely different level.

DESIGNERS AND DEVELOPERS: WHAT DO THEY DO AND WHICH DO I NEED?

Luckily, my first job after university was with an integrated agency, where I not only designed but also built websites. Although I no longer code, that experience gave me a great understanding from both the designer's and the developer's perspective.

In the early days of websites (when I started my career), you would have just used developers and designers. Now that technology has become more complex, and we expect more from digital content, specialist areas have developed within the web design world and - if you have the budget - you can have dedicated teams, each working on different areas of your website. Having worked on both the technical and creative sides, I have always been able to consider the whole project: how someone uses a site; can we actually build what would be the right kind of site for the client; and how do we make the design engaging and keep the user interested?

Nowadays, there tend to be User Experience teams (UX) who work with teams of Information Architects (IA). Some of their disciplines cross over, and while many of the larger digital agencies simply incorporate both roles under the umbrella of UX, I imagine they will become more defined and separate in the future as the technologies advance. There are then Designers or Visual Designers (VD) and teams of front and back-end developers. Below is an insight into who does what bit. I'm not going to go into any great depth, as that would mean writing an entire book for each! But, in the most basic terms, here is what each specialism does:

Information Architects (IA): They focus on the organisation and structure of the content to ensure the right information is presented in the right way, in the right place. An IA will develop wireframes (a line drawing of the website layout - a bit like plans you would have drawn up for a building) of where items should be placed on a website to enhance the experience. They will then organise and categorise the intended content for the website into a coherent structure. Good information architecture will enable the user to find what they are looking for quickly and make completing tasks easy.

User Experience Teams (UX): – They look at how the user interacts with a product or system and how the experience can be improved. This can cover everything from user testing and market research to interface design. Products such as iPhones and iPads are the best example of ease of use and efficiency. In terms of a website, the UX designer will get users to test the site and ensure the experience is as good as it can be. UX uses IA as its foundation, but takes it to the next level.

Designers or Visual Designers (VD): They will ensure all of the above is taken into consideration as they create the 'look and feel' for the website that is 'on brand' (working within the brand guidelines you supply) and appealing to the user (your target audience). They will look at what images work best to make the site aesthetically pleasing and consider what the buttons and other 'call to action' items should look like.

Developers/Coders: Will take the final files from the designer and build the fully-functional website or, if it's an app or new software, they will develop the final product using complex code.

Some UX/IA designers feel their job is more important than the VD's - and vice versa! In my opinion, both are of equal importance because if you have a site where everything is easy to find but the overall design does not inspire or capture your attention, the website has failed; the same applies if it's a beautifully designed website but you can't find what you're looking for.

Big corporates, such as HSBC and B&Q, will have a dedicated team for each area. That's not just because they have the budget, but also because their sites are normally so vast and they need to thoroughly test and research the ever-increasing numbers of new products and services they want to add.

For the smaller and medium-sized companies that need to outsource in the most cost-effective way, any good web design or multi-disciplined agency will make sure the team assigned to your project – no matter how small that team is - takes all the relevant elements into consideration. You just need to make sure you have briefed them properly and gone through your brand architecture, target audience and product or service with them in detail...and have chosen an agency that you're confident can deliver what you need...

WORKING IN TANDEM TO BE A SUCCESS

I can't stress enough how important it is to make sure you have good design and development teams. Some companies are stronger on the design side and some more on the technical side, but for a website to be truly successful you need both. To achieve this, you may have to enlist two separate companies and, if you do, then it's best to do it from the offset.

I've been approached by several companies who have enlisted a more technical team first and then fallen at the design stage, which has not only resulted in going over budget but also in deadlines having to be extended.

WaveTrax is a good example. They have created a new and very complex app, especially designed for people who enjoy sailing. They approached a specialist app development company who did a fantastic job with the app itself, but when it came to designing the website, although they were experts at coding such a site, they hadn't taken into account that it not only needed to explain what the app did, it also needed to be visually pleasing and - most importantly – actually sell the app.

Working with the client to understand what the app did, who it was targeting and what other ideas he had in mind for the future, enabled us to design a website that not only worked with the branding he'd already created, but also emphasised the main benefits of buying the app and made it easy for people to purchase it.

However, this redesign of the whole website meant the developers had to re-code the pages, so it not only took longer but also cost more than originally anticipated.

"As someone who has been involved in software for over 20 years, I thought it would simply be a case of giving my ideas on content and layout to a developer who would then code the site, give me some neat layout choices, build the website and take it live. It was a mistake that cost time and money, both of which could have been put to better use in the start up of my business.

I had a clear view on what needed to be communicated and my developer asked me, "What do you want it to look like?" In hindsight, that's where things started to go off the rails. I gave him sketches and PowerPoints and simply got back a cleaner version of what I'd designed. As the developer carried out every single aspect of change that I wanted to see, over a period of time I got an endless stream of revisions, as he kept adjusting and tuning the code to get as close as he could to what I was asking for.

Eventually, when I had the completed website, with all the pages, content, media, links and other functionality I wanted to see, I stood back and decided it simply didn't look right. That's when I realised that, despite all the effort from me and my developer, we were still missing the essential ingredient that means the difference between an average website that works and a cool site that presents visitors with a great experience: really creative design flair.

It was at that point, after I'd lost more than three months and a lot of money, that I turned to a specialised design agency, Beyond Creative Thinking. Their approach was not to do what they were told, but to take the framework of what I wanted to achieve, understand my business and then find a way to deliver what I wanted in a way that was unique but held true to the values and messages of the business.

All the design was done in graphic form, making changes very quick and easy, and it was only when I was happy with the final product that it was sent to the developer for coding and publishing. The agency liaised with the developer to ensure the coding work stuck to the plan and handled all the necessary adjustments.

Emma and her team gave me a bespoke, exciting interpretation of my business, using methods, media and a layout that sets our website apart from the others. They have produced a user-friendly, impressive and informative website that adds real value to the business. I wish I'd found them sooner!"

Paul Cuss, Founder and Managing Director, WaveTrax

Initial design created by the developers

New design with clear 'call to action' areas, information on the App and social media.

BankToTheFuture (BF) is another example of how not getting the website right at an early stage can cost time and money. I mentioned earlier how we worked with Simon Dixon to redesign his brand so that it properly represented his vision. However, the problems went further than simply the look and feel for the brand, as the website was already very far along in the development process, near completion. After looking at the design for the website, we both realised that not only would the new branding we were about to create change the look and feel of the website, but also that the current design contained a number of elements that would be frustrating from a user perspective.

"

WE'VE DONE IT THE WRONG WAY ROUND. I WISH I'D MET YOU EARLIER.

SIMON DIXON, CEO & CO-FOUNDER,
BANKTOTHEFUTURE.COM

"

But budgets were tight and a lot of money had already been spent. We decided to redesign the logo to incorporate their vision and to redesign the homepage to not only incorporate the new logo but to make it more user-friendly. As I explained in Chapter 3, BF has two target audiences - the investor and the entrepreneur/ business owner – and I felt it would be best to have a different video on the homepage for each audience, so the messages could be more targeted and hopefully lead to more conversions.

We had hoped the developers would be able to take the new design of the homepage and replicate the same look and feel throughout the website, to save on any extra design costs, but I ended up having to work closely with the team myself to achieve a consistent feel throughout. Further conversations with Simon led to the addition of some other ideas that would make the user's experience even better, so the whole project did end up costing BF considerably more than the original budget.

WHO IS MY WEBSITE FOR?

In order to be able to design a really effective website, you need to know who your audience is and how best to communicate with them. With the

Original designs created by the developers for BankToTheFuture

New designs following the rebranding for BankToTheFuture

technology market always changing, it's a good idea to know what mobile device(s) and platforms your particular target audience tends to use – for example, current research suggests that people in their early twenties tend to use BlackBerry. I recently worked on a project where users at one end of the audience scale would be using an iPad and at the other end quite a dated PC, so both needed to be considered for the project to be a success.

With the majority of people now using smart phones and tablets, it's important to make sure the various elements on your site will work on the different devices. iPhones and iPads still do not allow Flash, so if you want to have animation, e.g. rotating images, you might be better using JQuery, which is compatible on both iPhones and Android.

Also, rather than designing two different websites - one suitable for viewing on a smaller screen, such as a phone, and another for a computer monitor – look at whether you could have one site built using a 'responsive' layout. This is where the site automatically reconfigures its layout to work on the relevant device, and it's compatible across all platforms. Not every website can work in this way, but it's worth considering. Although using HTML5 allows for some innovative ideas, it still has issues on IE9 (Internet Explorer 9).

USING BEHAVIOURAL TARGETING

Behavioural targeting is where a website tracks what you do while you're browsing - such as which adverts you click on, the products you look at and how much you spend - and builds a profile of your shopping habits. This approach personalises shoppers' experiences when they visit your site, gives you a great insight into what your customers want and should result in increased sales. Amazon uses it and now Tesco Direct has adopted the same approach, with a multi-million pound initiative. Due to the cost, it's not the route every company can currently afford to follow, but it seems to be the direction retail websites are taking.

This major shift will move the website from 'manual merchandising' to an automatic, algorithmically-merchandised offer, which means the content will be driven by recommendations and data feeds about topics such as sales and top products. Tesco is integrating its Clubcard, allowing customers to see content that reflects both their purchases and purchases made by customers

Example of the responsive Beyond Creative Thinking website on an
iPhone and desktop computer (see it working by activating the image)

with similar profiles. Tesco is also adding thousands of extra non-food items to its website each month - another reason for them to change how the site worked.

A loyalty card, such as the Tesco Clubcard, can give valuable information to a brand about its customers: shopping habits and preferences, household income, travel habits, how charitable you are and what competitions and promotions are appealing to you. This information can then be used to target individual consumers, to make their shopping experience more relevant and - most importantly - to get them to spend more.

THE PURPOSE OF YOUR WEBSITE

You need to know who you are, what you're selling and have a clear vision for your website. If its sole purpose is to sell products, you need a very good e-commerce site that's easy to navigate and visually pleasing. Your design team need to think not only about the homepage, but also the process of how a user searches for and buys an item and how they are taken through the checkout process. As a rule, once they're in the checkout process, the main navigation should disappear so that they can focus on paying.

Some websites need to be very creative, especially (without wishing to state the obvious) if you're in a creative industry. Experiments such as the HTML5 experiment 'The Wilderness Downtown' - create a great user experience and help the web evolve.

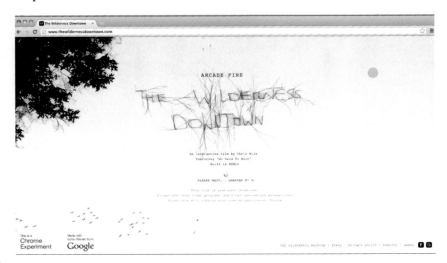

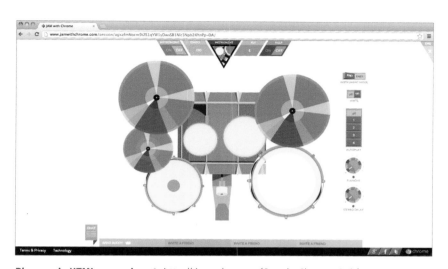

Play music HTML5 experiment: http://tiny.cc/vqyrsw (Google Chrome Only)

Blow up a video HTML5 experiment:
http://tiny.cc/etyrsw (Google Chrome Only)

OPPOSITE
The Wilderness Downtown HTML5 experiment
www.thewildernessdowntown.com (Google Chrome Only)

MAKING YOUR WEBSITE USER FRIENDLY

As we live in such a complex world full of so much choice, we don't spend hours reading websites; we're more likely to just scan and pick out the bits that catch our eye or are relevant to what we're looking for. And if we can't find it quickly, we move on to the next website, and so on, until we have found it.

> **THE FIRST TEN SECONDS OF A PAGE VISIT ARE CRITICAL TO THE USER'S DECISION TO STAY OR LEAVE.**
>
> (MICROSOFT RESEARCH)

This is why it's so important to understand your market and what those people might be looking for, and to be clear on what you want them to understand about you. Having a very clear tagline that underpins what you do, positioned in a suitable place on your homepage, will help people decide if they're visiting the right site. Then it's about the information you give them.

Writing for the web is very different to writing for print. On the web, you need to reduce the amount of copy compared to print, keep it as relevant as possible and pull out key items to attract people's attention. Reducing the copy results in more white space, which allows the important bits to stand out so that visitors can clearly see what they're looking for.

Think about what your visitor really wants to know – the nuts and bolts – and that's what you need to put on your homepage. You can add more detailed pages where appropriate but have the extra information as an extra if they want it, rather than clogging up every page with endless text. Going back to the Tuttoluxo example in Chapter 2, the client wanted detailed information on each product but, after speaking to the potential customers of the site, we discovered that this was something only the professional beauticians would want to know, not the everyday customer. This resulted in them displaying short information next to each product with more detailed information as a click option.

HOW MANY CLICKS?

Some people say your customer must be able to access the information they need within two clicks but with some sites now being so large, this can be difficult. It's more important to make each click more relevant and easy for the customer to go back if they wish.

I recently worked on a site where you had a homepage that only gave you two options; it then took you to another page with a further two options; only on the third click did you finally get to what really should have been the homepage. The site was only a year old and it had been built this way because the company was going to have several divisions. Even if it had gone ahead with those divisions, the site would still have been very annoying for the user, so it was reworked and a lot of extra elements to engage the user were introduced, such as more videos and a more logical format to the pages.

Keeping things simple will make the experience much easier for the user - you don't want them to overthink or have to question every button they need to click. You might think you're being 'different' by re-naming well-understood buttons, such as changing 'search' to 'keyword', but this means the user will have to think for longer than they should. If you want to be different, do it in other ways, such as through your choice of imagery and videos or having a design that stands out from your competitors.

Steve Krug is a Web Usability Expert and author of the book, 'Don't make me think', and this excerpt from his book is just one example of how people use the web in different ways:

'...people will type a site's entire URL into the Yahoo search box every time they want to go there – not just to find the site for the first time, but every time they want to go there, sometimes several times a day. If you ask them about it, it becomes clear that some of them think that Yahoo is the internet, and that this is the way you use it.'

So, when designing your site, not only do you need to bear in mind what kind of device your target audience will use to view your website, you also need to be aware of the different levels of understanding they might have of the online world.

MAKING THE USER THINK

Lots of elements on a website can make a user stop and think unnecessarily or make a simple task take longer than needed. Below are a few examples of how the user's experience can be improved.

Two simple 'Call to Action' buttons

DONATE NOW

HELP OUR APPEAL

OBVIOUS
The button instantly tells the user they can make a donation.

CONFUSING
The button is misleading. It could mean it allows the user to make a donation or it might take them to a page where they can find out about different ways to help the charity.

A simple task
I've experienced this on a few websites. The user gets a nice little box in which to type their query or description and is either told at the beginning that the user has a limited number of characters or is told once they click the 'submit' button.

Filling out the form correctly requires the user to either guess the number of characters they have written and keep clicking the 'submit' button or type the response in another programme which will count the characters and then simply cut and paste. These solutions all take time and will annoy the user.

Please provide a brief description.
Text must be no longer than 250 characters *

Please provide a brief description.
Text must be no longer than 250 characters *

43 characters left

Solution
The problem could easily be resolved by either:

■ Not limiting the amount of characters (although not always ideal)
■ Adding a simple Javascript counter which informs the user how many characters they have left

DO I NEED TO TEST?

The short answer is: yes! It's always a good idea to test your website and it doesn't have to cost vast amounts of money. Of course, if your site is only going to have a few pages, then it may not be necessary, but larger websites, especially e-commerce sites, certainly need to have some testing.

Testing a website doesn't involve a focus group – those are used to gain feedback on products or get opinions – it simply consists, in its most basic form, of one person using the site with another person observing and taking notes. Generally, you will devise a set of tasks you want the user to perform, such as finding a certain product or piece of information, signing up to the newsletter or going through the purchase process.

Some larger companies will have two versions of their homepage created and test to see which generates the most sales. They will also test their sites using an operation room with a one-way mirror, so that the tester doesn't feel as self-conscious as they might with someone sitting beside them.

If you have the budget, you could recruit several people that match your target market. However, if money is tight, then using someone who simply understands the internet will still give you an idea of how people will use your site.

If any issues come to light, then it's a good idea to test again once you've made the amendments, to make sure the problem has been resolved. Depending on the type of site you're creating, you may need to test throughout the process.

With the Tuttoluxo site, the client simply got someone from another company in the same building to use the old and new websites to see which was easier. Luckily for me, the new site won hands down!

HAVE A PLAN AND GET THE RIGHT PEOPLE ON BOARD

The process for building a website depends on your budget and the type of website you need. Here is a basic outline, but bear in mind that each of these steps can have several branches to them, depending on the size and complexity of the site and the type of design/development and agency you use:

1: Have in place a clear brand and vision you're happy with

2: Know your audience

3: Decide what type of website you think you need

4: Approach suitable web design/development companies

5: Work with the designer and developer or user experience designer (UX) to create a suitable site map showing the hierarchy and organisation of the information required for your website

6: Discuss what kind of content management system (CMS) will be created, to allow you to add and amend content yourself in the 'back end' of the site

7: Depending on the type of website, you may need wireframes to be created

8: Again, depending on the size of your website, you may need an interactive wireframe created so the user experience can be tested

9: The homepage look and feel will then be created and you'll need to consider the images, video and copy that will be used

10: The chosen design of the homepage will then be taken across the remaining pages

11: Once approved, this then gets passed to the developer, who will start building and testing the site

12: All the content - images, copy, etc. - gets added once the site is built

13: Once a final test has been completed, the site can go live

It may sound like a long process, but it's all logical and should prevent you from having to start again halfway through, as BankToTheFuture.com and WaveTrax had to.

THAT'S NOT THE END...

Once your site is up and running, make sure you don't allow it to get out of date – don't waste all the money and time you've spent on it so far! Regularly updating the copy, blog and news, together with refreshing offers and adding new products, will keep users coming back and means Google will like it more.

And don't forget to make sure your website is part of your email and social media campaigns – with landing pages for promotions and events, etc. - as this will help drive traffic.

In short, if you're going to have a website built, do the job properly and enlist the right people at the right time, or it could cost you both time and money. A website isn't something that can be built in a few days; it can take several months to create a small site from start to finish and years to create complex ones, such as the large e-commerce sites that have thousands of products. With more and more people communicating digitally and understanding the web on a much higher level than ever before, you will be judged harshly if your site isn't fit for purpose - and you could lose customers.

"The new website Beyond Creative Thinking designed and built helps position Ropewalk as one of the country's leading destinations for shoppers, particularly the fashion-conscious family, who can now purchase their favourite clothing, either casual or smart, in one convenient shopping trip. Visitors to the website can keep up to date with all the latest offers from our retailers, as well as news of events."

John Kelleher, Ropewalk Centre Manager

www.ropewalknuneaton.co.uk

THE DIGITAL REVOLUTION: SO MUCH MORE THAN 'SOCIAL MEDIA'...

FIRST, THE WEBSITE ARRIVED AND MILLIONS OF COMPANIES JUMPED ON THE BANDWAGON, 'KNOCKING THEM UP' WITHOUT MUCH THOUGHT, WHICH RESULTED IN A FLOOD OF UNSIGHTLY AND UN-USER-FRIENDLY WEBSITES. NOW ALL I HEAR IS PEOPLE TALKING ABOUT SOCIAL MEDIA AND HOW THEIR COMPANY NEEDS A FACEBOOK AND TWITTER ACCOUNT, BUT THERE'S VERY LITTLE UNDERSTANDING OF WHAT THEY REALLY ARE AND WHETHER THEY WILL ADD ANY BENEFIT.

THROUGH THE RISE OF 'SOCIAL MEDIA EXPERTS' GIVING SEMINARS AND ONE-TO-ONE COACHING, PEOPLE CAN LEARN TO USE A SELECTION OF THE VAST NUMBER OF SOCIAL MEDIA PLATFORMS OUT THERE VERY EFFECTIVELY, BUT THERE'S STILL VERY LITTLE TALK OR INFORMATION ABOUT ALL THE OTHER EXCITING THINGS HAPPENING IN THE DIGITAL ARENA THAT CAN ADD HUGE VALUE TO YOUR TOTAL BRAND EXPERIENCE AND KEEP YOU RIGHT ON TREND. AND, FOR DESIGNERS LIKE ME, IT MEANS WE CAN NOW BE EVEN MORE CREATIVE IN DIFFERENT AREAS AND SPREAD PEOPLE'S BRANDS ACROSS EVEN MORE PLATFORMS. WE ARE IN VERY EXCITING TIMES!

I WON'T GO INTO GREAT DEPTH AND DISCUSS THE EXACT TECHNOLOGY BEHIND THESE VARIOUS DIGITAL OPTIONS; I JUST WANT YOU TO UNDERSTAND A LITTLE ABOUT WHAT'S CURRENTLY OUT THERE - SOME OF WHICH YOU MAY ALREADY HAVE HEARD OF - AND THAT IT'S NOT ALL ABOUT FACEBOOK, TWITTER AND EMAIL CAMPAIGNS.

I'm going to start with something I think is really exciting. You may already have tried out some of the samples in this book, but if you don't know anything about Augmented Reality, here goes.

AUGMENTED REALITY (AR)

This is a fantastic new development and can really get the user involved with your brand. Using the appropriate application (app), the user simply holds their smartphone or tablet over an AR image or object to activate the content and bring it to life. The huge advantage of AR is it doesn't have to redirect you to another site to play the footage – it animates right there and then, using the app technology. You can make 2D images 3D, so if you hold your phone or tablet over a 2D image of a map, the technology will turn it into an interactive 3D version and, with a tap of your finger on the screen, you can make the 3D version perform different functions. I think it's truly incredible.

Although it was originally seen as a gimmick, I believe this is going to revolutionise print, and mixing it with direct mail, viral campaigns, packaging and events will add a whole new level to campaigns and keep them well-balanced from a consumption point of view.

AR has wrap-around and three-dimensional recognition capabilities (whereas QR codes are only two-dimensional - see the next section), which is perfect for making products or objects at an event or in-store interactive, allowing consumers to either buy instantly via their phone or be taken to other information. You can even program the app to take the user to different offers, depending on the time of day they activate the picture or object. The technology has even been used in food posters at train stations, enabling the customer to buy shopping while waiting to catch the train to work in the morning.

(The only downside I have found so far is that you need to have an app to allow you to use the technology and it can take time to register with iTunes, whereas you can instantly generate QR codes yourself via a multitude of sites.)

If you didn't download the BeyondCT App for your smart phone when you started this book, simply download it now via your app store (for instructions on how to use the app see page 9).

There are various ways the technology can be used; some light-hearted and others more serious. Here are a few examples of companies using AR to enhance their brand experience:

Cadbury added AR to their wrappers in the run-up to the Olympics. When you photographed the wrapper with your smartphone, the 'Quaksmak' app, devised by Blipper, recognised the wrapper in a similar manner to a QR code (without a big, ugly square ruining the design) and took you to a game, which was part of the brand's 'Spots V Stripes' Olympics activity. The player chose to be a 'Spot' or 'Stripe', before ducks appeared from either side of the chocolate bar. They had to 'smack' the opposing team's ducks by tapping the screen. The app was compatible with Apple and Android handsets.

Rayban Virtual Mirror uses AR. This allows you to try on the entire range of Rayban glasses from your very own computer. I think as technology improves this will be adopted by more online retail sites.

Tesco AR poster in South Korea allows commuters to purchase shopping while on the move. The items are delivered to their homes later in the day.

Business cards can be brought to life with AR. This could eventually replace the boring (and unsightly – yes, I'm going to keep saying it!) QR codes that people have started to put on their cards. Rather than just a video of a head talking a more creative block effect has been used. I think this gives a good idea of where the technology could take us.

A BMW Z4 on your desk! was one of the first to allow you to take an AR model in your hands, place it on your desktop and then control the car from the keyboard and webcam while you drove it around your desk! You could also save the graphic you had created and share with your friends on Facebook & Twitter.

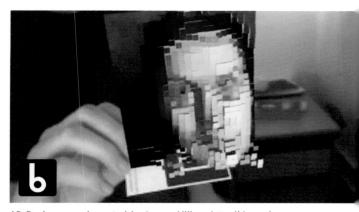

AR Business card created by James Alliban http://tiny.cc/oxyrsw

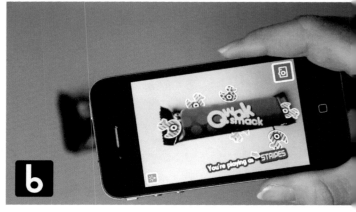

AR Cadbury wrapper activates the game Spots V Stripes

Film teasers. Warner Bros. used AR to create an interactive campaign for the launch of the Sherlock Holmes film. The app directed people to 'The Game of Shadows' when they took pictures of the national poster campaign or newspaper articles. Esquire magazine featured an AR cover that not only activated the film trailer but also featured Robert Downey Jr. explaining AR.

It was also used in the Green Lantern film campaign and unlocked audio samples and visual animations. The two films used the app 'Zappar' to enable the AR.

Sherlock Holmes AR poster: http://tiny.cc/1rb4sw
AR Esquire cover video: http://tiny.cc/qsb4sw

Heinz ketchup. Heinz ketchup. Rather than attaching a small fold-out booklet to their bottles, Heinz have used an AR label that activates an AR recipe book, which the customer can then download. Not only does that mean the customer can't lose the recipes, but it's also easier for Heinz to update them without incurring extra print costs.

Heinz Ketchup AR video: http://tiny.cc/qtb4sw

QUICK RESPONSE CODES (QR CODES)

These are single colour, square graphics made up of a series of shapes (usually squares). If you download a barcode reader onto your phone, the phone can scan the image and take you to the web domain associated with the graphic. They are a great alternative to having to add a very long URL to a design and have made it possible for printed items to interact with the digital world, allowing us to create campaigns that are truly multi-platform. But QR codes can be temperamental from a scanning perspective and I don't like them, aesthetically, from a design point of view.

I know that these days they don't all have to be made of just a series of squares and that some brands like Ted Baker have customised theirs to make them more interesting, but the truth is they take up a large amount of space, as you have to make them big enough for the phone sensors to pick up the detail to connect you to the URL. However, on the plus side, they can be read by any smartphone that has the app.

The online betting brand, Betfair, placed QR codes on the bikini bottoms of two beach volleyball players during the test Olympics tournament. When the codes were photographed by a smartphone, the user was redirected to a registration page to join Betfair and offered a free bet.

Oxfam used QR codes on their clothes tags in one of their London stores. When users scanned the QR code, a video would play a short movie from the celebrity who used to own the particular garment, talking about where they wore it, etc.

QR codes are also being used in practical applications within the technology sector. If you ever feel the need to take your computer apart, you will notice that nearly every component has a QR code on it.

OPPOSITE: QR code used to advertise Betfair at the beach volleyball

ALTERNATIVES TO QR CODES

Technology is always advancing and we are always trying to improve what we currently have. That applies to QR codes; love them or hate them, there are alternatives available:

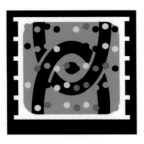

Microsoft tag. MS Tag is similar to a QR code in that it scans 2D objects and directs you to a URL but, unlike the QR code, it can be printed in multiple colours and put together in a much more creative way. The downside is that it currently only supports iPhones.

Mobile Visual Search (MVS). You take a picture with your phone's camera and it then searches like a search engine and feeds back relevant links/information associated with that picture. Your smartphone still needs to download an app to allow your camera to do this but, as technology advances, I'm sure it will become an integral part of phones and will be used for finding all sorts of content - such as images stored on our computers - rather than typing what we require in a search bar. There are a few companies already adopting this search technology, the most well-known being Google Goggles.

So why not look into how you might be able to use AR, QR codes and MVS to enhance your brand? Just don't forget to let your customers know that they can now use this technology to interact with you!

APPS

Everyone's heard of apps and they can add another dimension to your business, as long as you make sure they're relevant and add real value to your customer. Spending huge amounts of money on a game (and everyone loves Angry Birds), while it might be fun and engaging, certainly won't add value to every business. On the other hand, creating an app where people can quickly browse and buy your products will not only add value but should also increase revenue. Sometimes apps can actually be a more effective way of interacting with your customers - for example, eBay's app is easier to use than their website, as it has 'one click' processing.

Again, to ensure apps translate into business success, the same rules apply as in traditional media: you need to understand your audience, have your brand clearly in place and then you need a good designer and developer on board, just as you would for a website. And you must make sure the app and your website are in sync with each other and are developed together, so you don't fall into the same trap as WaveTrax did (see previous chapter), where the functionality of the app worked well, but the site didn't take into consideration the brand or the audience and failed to emphasise the key benefits of the app to drive sales.

A QUICK REMINDER:

When creating apps, using MVS or sending video clips, remember that there are restrictions on certain devices, e.g. iPhones won't allow you to view Flash files. You may need to develop more than one version or compromise to create something that works across all smartphones.

USING VIDEO

In the days of dial-up, streaming video or watching your favourite TV show over the internet would have been unthinkable. But today, with high-speed broadband and the likes of YouTube and Vimeo, online video is now very easily accessible and can quickly deliver high-impact messages while retaining the attention of the visitor far more effectively than pages of copy.

YouTube is now the second largest search engine after Google, with 60 hours of video being uploaded every minute and over 4 billion videos being viewed each day. With these kinds of statistics, it clearly makes sense to invest in video. Google likes

> **IN JULY 2012, AN AVERAGE MALE IN THE UK SPENT 40.6 HOURS WATCHING ONLINE VIDEOS, DOUBLE THE 19.0 HOURS FOR AN AVERAGE FEMALE.**
>
> SEPTEMBER 7, 2012
> WWW.COMSCOREDATAMINE.COM

websites with video content, and communicating messages via embedded videos makes visiting your site a much more engaging experience for the user.

Video can also extend way beyond just your website or YouTube; you need to look at how the wider audience is communicating and create that two-way stream wherever you can. 500 years of YouTube video is watched every day on Facebook and over 700 YouTube videos are shared on Twitter each minute. That's a heck of a lot of video footage! If you can encourage your audience to 'like', 'share', or comment on your video, it'll help spread your brand more widely, and with 100 million people taking social actions on YouTube every week, it seems silly not to create a video and engage with them.

I'm currently working with a very interesting client to create an online training website for a very specific market and the majority of the content will be video, as it's certainly the best way to deliver the right experience for their users.

And if you think there's no point creating a video for your brand because your target audience is 'too old', not only to watch video online but to 'surf the net', think again!

AMONG INTERNET USERS AGED 50-64, SOCIAL NETWORKING SITE USAGE ON A TYPICAL DAY GREW A SIGNIFICANT 60% (FROM 20% TO 32%)

MARY MADDEN, KATHRYN ZICKUHR
AUG 26, 2011

Video is being used in a variety of ways to attract very different audiences and to bring people closer to their brands. The website www.joyus.com is a beauty website that heavily uses video to demonstrate and sell its products online. Personally, I don't think it's a very good-looking site, but the idea behind it is very interesting.

The creative ideas behind some videos have resulted in campaigns 'going viral' and taking the brands global, for example:

The Tipp-Ex viral is a very creative and interactive campaign. The user watches a short clip called 'A hunter shoots a bear', during which the hunter decides he doesn't really want to shoot the bear, so he reaches out of the video box, grabs the Tipp-Ex and removes the word 'shoots' from the title. You can then type what you would like to see the hunter do to the bear. Whatever the user types in the box then loads a video, which plays the scenario.

This viral received 6,855,877 views in just two weeks and bloggers had even been giving tips on what you could make the hunter do to the bear, such as 'tickles', 'paints' and 'eats'.

Tipp-Ex - A hunter shoots a bear!: http://youtu.be/4ba1BqJ4S2M

Little Gordon is one of my favourite examples of creative video going viral. There are several different videos, each featuring 'Little Gordon', a child who is acting out different scenarios, pretending to be a young Gordon Ramsey – and the mannerisms and scripts are just perfect. The videos were produced to promote a catering company and spread so quickly and successfully that a US TV programme even showed a clip while they were interviewing the real Gordon Ramsey. He liked them so much that he now often plays them himself at cooking events where he's demonstrating!

Rabbit campaign: I created the concept for this campaign in 2011 to coincide with Easter, as a fun promotion for my own company. The video was a simple animation containing two rabbits, doing what rabbits do best! This then led into the point of the video. We had a censored and an uncensored version, to help engage for longer with the audience - it was quite amazing to see how many people actually clicked to view the uncensored version!

Little Gordon viral video campaign: http://youtu.be/WcZqwR9tbJE

IT DOESN'T ALWAYS HAVE TO COST THOUSANDS...

Although having a professional video created will look stunning, you can easily film testimonials using your own video camera and upload them to your website and YouTube page - just make sure you have good lighting and sound and a decent backdrop. Video testimonials are not only more engaging than written ones, but seeing the person talking also makes them more believable.

PLAN, PLAN AND PLAN YOUR VIDEO.

There are a lot of video companies to choose from and they all have different pricing structures and levels of creativity. Make sure you look at samples they have created before and understand exactly how they work. For example, will they provide you with a storyboard of how the final product will look and, after they've shot the video, are they going to go through the clips they plan on using before they start creating the final product?

When choosing suppliers, in my opinion, the well-known phrase: 'if you pay peanuts you get monkeys', is very true, so make sure you understand what you are getting and what you're not getting.

And if you're able to plan ahead for content you might need to use in the future, you could save money by getting all the footage at one time. For example, part of the Zepter International brand experience campaign I created included attending the BBC Good Food Show and not only demonstrating their products using two top chefs, but also shooting footage of the event and testimonials to use on their website, in email campaigns and on YouTube. In the near future, we also planned to add some close-up demonstrations of the cookware. Rather than having to organise several video shoots and paying to hire chefs, a camera crew and a venue at a later date, we simply shot everything we knew we would need for the next 6-12 months while at the show. From the two-day shoot, we ended up with 10 hours of video, which would more than cover the next six months.

Rabbit Easter campaign for Beyond Creative Thinking: http://tiny.cc/vlzrsw

PROJECTION MAPPING

This adds great impact to a brand and is far more attention grabbing than a billboard. It works by mapping three-dimensional points to a two-dimensional plane. An animation or video is then created to work within the area and projected onto the object of choice, such as a building. The projections not only act as a huge advert but interact with live audiences and passers-by. The technique allows brands to create worlds that wouldn't normally exist, like buildings appearing to be crumbling down or people appearing inside windows.

These spectacular projections are often filmed by passers-by on their smartphones and instantly uploaded to YouTube, which helps spread brands globally and encourages consumers to interact further with them.

A COUPLE OF EXAMPLES:

Toyota Auris Hybrid: As Toyota demonstrates perfectly, this new form of technology can be projected onto anything. The Toyota campaign message, 'Get your energy back', is in reference to the Auris hybrid technology that recycles the energy while you drive.

Toyota Projection Mapping: http://youtu.be/UJ7E7uEZNoo

Virgin Money Senate House 3D Projection: **Virgin** is always looking at ways of making things better and, to celebrate their new quest into banking, Richard Branson hosted the official launch with a 270 degree, fully immersive, architectural projection on the University of London's Senate House Library. The inspiration for the projection came from their '40 Years of Better' TV advert.

Virgin Money Projection Mapping: http://youtu.be/OUYQxSU7Abk

EMAIL CAMPAIGNS

Although this has become a very saturated form of communication - and with enhanced spam filters it's even harder to get your emails through - it's a tried and tested marketing tool that can still work, if done correctly. One thing I have found works particularly well these days is keeping it as short and to the point as possible. People are so busy and tend to receive such a lot of emails that the more concise you can make it, the more able and likely they are to read it and to make a quick decision as to whether it's for them.

For example, the Easter campaign video I mentioned earlier was sent as both a direct mail item and also an email campaign. To test the theory around long versus short emails, two versions were sent to a cold mailing list: one looked like the usual email-style newsletter containing some information about the company and a link to the video; the second simply looked like a personal email, addressed to the recipient, along with a few short lines about the video and my usual footer signature. The long version had a 15% open rate and the shorter version had a 47% open rate. Point proven.

You cannot currently embed video into an email and have the recipient play it via their inbox; instead you send an image or link which clicks through to the video on YouTube or wherever you've uploaded it. It's important to state in your brief message how long the video is, so people know how much time they're going to have to 'give up' to watch it.

The following is a particularly clever way of using email and video. Virgin sent an email to everyone taking part in the London 2012 Marathon and when you clicked the link it played a video which mentioned the participant by name. Of course, this could then be posted on Facebook, etc. and who isn't going to post a video that mentions them?!

Although we can send emails that take the consumer to a captivating video, and it's very cost effective, I think email still has a lot to learn from direct mail. While you can split your database and send different emails to different demographics, what some of the email systems allow is still nowhere near as advanced as what can be achieved with direct mail.

MIXING SOCIAL MEDIA AND TECHNOLOGY WITH RETAIL SHOPPING

With more consumers buying online than ever before, retailers need to work harder to entice people into high street stores. Although QR codes have been adopted by some – such as Oxfam, who added them to clothes tags – we, as consumers, always have a thirst for more and, with such an interconnected world, retailers need to devise new ways to engage with customers.

The Republic retail store is trialling a virtual mirror, 'MiMirror', which uses ground-breaking technology that allows consumers to see how garments will suit them, without physically trying them on. Although this certainly adds a new, fun dimension to 'the shopping experience', you do still need to try clothes on at some point, so I can't see it ever replacing the changing room! But the device certainly has a PR function, as it also allows the consumer to 'share' pictures of themselves in the clothes. This could drive sales, as friends can give their opinion on the items, but - most importantly - it spreads the brand's name and products.

FACEBOOK SYNCHRONIZATION SYSTEM

Ushuaia Ibiza Beach hotel, a luxury property on the Balearic island, claims to be the first hotel to offer a Facebook synchronisation system. Guests can be provided with a wristband, which is synchronised with their Facebook profile. Facebook 'pillars' are set up throughout the hotel, where guests can check in, take pictures or post a status with just a swipe of their wristband over the sensors. Whether people are that keen to have their every move documented remains to be seen...

MAKING DIGITAL SOCIAL

Using social media not only helps you interact with your audience and spread your brand, it also allows your digital campaigns to be shared and liked. But remember, the same rules still apply: be clear on what your brand is trying to say, its values and vision, who your audience is and the best time of day to post. The tone of voice you created at the beginning needs to be brought right through to your social media and don't be tempted to simply push your brand. Consumers want a two-way relationship, so focus on interacting and giving them some real value.

> 53% OF TWITTER USERS RE-TWEET MATERIAL POSTED BY OTHERS, WITH 18% DOING SO ON A DAILY BASIS.
>
> AARON SMITH, SENIOR RESEARCH SPECIALIST AND LEE RAINIE, DECEMBER 9, 2010

Not all social media will suit your company, as your customers will use different platforms to communicate. Facebook, for example, works quite well with retail – when it was used as part of an integrated campaign for the beauty brand Tuttoluxo, we had 800 clicks on their website in one day (the advert cost £25). You need to go back to your target market research and find out what kinds of social media your customers tend to engage with.

You don't have to spend hours on social media each day in order to make it worthwhile. Tools such as Hootsuite allow you to schedule your posts to go out at different times of the day on different days and you can easily add posts in between meetings via your smartphone.

Getting the whole team involved will also help get your brand out there, although you will need to set guidelines to ensure the messages are consistent. Make sure everyone understands the tone of voice you want to use and how long you want them to spend posting and responding to messages and tweets (you don't want them to be online all day and neglect what they're really meant to be doing!) There is also a lot of talk at the moment about building your 'personal brand', so allowing your staff to post about the company will ensure you are top of the game.

"What made me finally 'get' social media was one of my tweets being picked up, via LinkedIn, by an editor of a Sunday Paper who wanted to do a two-page feature on Peace One Day, the charity for which I'm president of the Patrons programme. I set myself a goal of mastering social media and the web in 2012 and I've made good progress. I can't believe how easy it all is once you learn it, and as long as you're clear on your outcomes and trust the process, it delivers - for sure."

Steve Bolton, Founding Partner, Platinum Partners

When used properly, social media certainly does deliver, but here's a gentle warning that it can go wrong if you're not careful...

Toyota may have ticked all the boxes with projection mapping, but their attempt at a viral campaign didn't go so well. The campaign consisted of you signing up an unknowing friend to receive prank calls, emails, texts and letters. Anyone who thinks this might have been a good idea will need to re-evaluate after reading about the woman who was led to believe she was being stalked by a dangerous man and subsequently sued Toyota for $10m. Although it's hard to imagine a campaign going much more wrong than this, as Toyota doubtless received a lot of press around the time of this story, maybe it wasn't all bad news!

But while you need to be aware of all the possible consequences of a viral campaign and prepare your brand accordingly, the truth is that, as long as you do your research properly, it could be the biggest and best viral campaign yet.

> # ONE OF THE BIGGEST CHANGES DIGITIZATION HAS BROUGHT IS THAT NO ELEMENT OF A BRAND OR CAMPAIGN STANDS ALONE ANYMORE. EACH PART FEEDS INTO THE OTHERS, AND BRANDS HAVE TO BE READY TO RESPOND AND ADAPT ON THE FLY.
>
> MELANIE MAY, MARKETING MAGAZINE, AUG 2011

MIX YOUR MEDIA CREATIVELY TO ENGAGE WITH YOUR AUDIENCE

Mixing different media - whether digital, traditional or both - to engage creatively with your audience can really create a 'total experience' of your brand.

L'Oreal launched an integrated campaign called 'Men Expert', which was a shift from its usual celebrity-led marketing strategy. The campaign had a touch of Bond about it - a dash of irony with some clever quips - and it integrated nicely into social media. It was to target men who were unfamiliar with L'Oreal's male grooming sub-brands and used a character called 'The Expert' to showcase its range. The campaign ran across YouTube and Facebook and was supported by an iPhone app.

The Expert appeared in four humorous 'how to...' videos that demonstrated the best way to tie a tie, pick a lock, take a profile picture and choose a mobile app. The UK and Ireland Facebook pages allowed consumers to ask him questions by 'liking' the page.

"The Expert quadrupled 'likes' of the L'Oreal Men Expert Facebook page and increased engagement with those on the page tenfold, while also receiving more views on YouTube than anything else L'Oreal had ever published – in short, he did the job he was created to do. But, more importantly, The Expert enabled L'Oreal to change as an organisation; he led them away from the comfort of traditional media to play in the brave new world of digital, and, significantly, he ripped up L'Oreal's internal rule book and encouraged the brand to take itself less seriously. It's that change in organisational behaviour that will be The Expert's lasting heritage."

Stuart Hogg, Account Director at VCCP, who created 'The Expert'.

WHAT NEXT...?

We are in exciting times and the technology in both traditional and digital media is only going to improve as we strive for perfection and each form of media continues to compete against the other to stay ahead in the game. It does make the lives of business owners, marketing professionals and those of us in the creative industry slightly difficult, as we're always trying to keep up with the latest developments, but that's progress.

If you're just starting on the journey of using multiple media streams to engage people with your brand, or you've tried a little but want to take it to the next level, just remember the basics of understanding who your brand is and who your audience is, then be creative. There's no point spending time and money working out what platforms and technologies to use if your campaign isn't engaging, creative and if your brand isn't fully in place. Get the right experts in at the right time, research, plan and then get it out there!

STAND UP AND STAND OUT:
MAKING THE MOST OF EXHIBITIONS

EXHIBIT, *NOUN,* TO PRESENT FOR OTHERS TO SEE

EXHIBITIONS AREN'T JUST PLACES YOU 'HAVE' TO GO TO, OR 'JOLLIES' FOR THE TEAM; YOU NEED TO VIEW EVERY EVENT YOUR BRAND ATTENDS AS A FANTASTIC OPPORTUNITY TO STAND OUT AND ENGAGE WITH YOUR AUDIENCE — OTHERWISE WHAT'S THE POINT IN BEING THERE?

DO YOUR HOMEWORK

Attending shows and exhibitions can be relatively expensive, so it's essential to carry out some due diligence before you commit. Visit the shows you're interested in first and ask exhibitors what their experience of the show is – most people are happy to speak honestly. Also, note where people accumulate, as you will find there are certain 'hotspots'. At one show I attended, I noticed the majority of visitors walked straight past all the stalls near the entrance because they were focused on 'getting in'. Speak to the organisers as well - they can usually provide very good statistics on the demographics of attendees and the footfall.

DON'T BOTHER IF YOU'RE NOT GOING TO MAKE THE EFFORT!

I've been to a huge number of exhibitions over the years and always find it interesting (and slightly depressing) how un-engaging some stands are. It's usually the companies who have chosen shell schemes that make the least amount of effort. They tend to stick up a couple of badly-designed, uninformative posters on the back panels, or have had some inexpensive pull-up banners made, and the people supposed to be manning the stand are either sat in a chair playing on their mobile, or they've disappeared entirely, creating a terrible impression of the brand: that it's not worth bothering with. This attitude and approach is just good money wasted.

It doesn't have to cost a huge amount to make your stand a little more engaging and smiles are free! Having well-designed graphics and looking for more unusual ways to present your brand can make a huge difference. Plan for the future - for example, rather than spending a fortune hiring a stool and table at every show you attend, why not buy something, as it will probably save you money in the long run.

GROW YOUR STAND OVER TIME

There are lots of different display and presentation systems on the market at the moment; some are more suited to space-only areas and some work with shell schemes. Some of the modular systems allow you to reconfigure the same stand into different sizes, which makes it perfect if you're going to be booking spaces of varying sizes throughout the year. Modular systems can also be added too, so you can start small and grow as your business grows.

(Just bear in mind that if you plan to purchase one of the systems where you can reconfigure the shape, you need to ensure the graphics for each panel will allow for this - or have more than one set of panels printed.)

If you're not sure whether you are going to attend events regularly, then you can always hire the stand displays and furnishings the first time and then buy if you decide to attend more events. BlueSquare Data hired their exhibition stand first time around, as we wanted to see whether the event was worth attending in the future. It was a shell scheme, so we designed the stand to fit into the space and the graphics were stored in case we attended another show. The Tuttoluxo branded marquee was also hired the first time it was used, which fitted perfectly into the branding budget and the overall marketing plan, which was only at the stage of testing the market.

If you have a larger budget and opt for 'space only', you can be more creative and, the larger the budget, the more gadgets you can add, to make it more visually appealing and a more interactive experience for the visitors. Parago had been attending the BETT show for a number of years and wanted to up their game. The brief was to create a stand that was very open and would make people remember the brand. The show itself is very compact and each year, as they squeeze more stands in, the walkways become narrower. As most of the surrounding stands were heavily enclosed, it was certainly important to make their stand open, to make them instantly different, and the large 'O's', which could be seen from quite a distance, made the brand more visible and memorable.

GETTING YOUR AUDIENCE ONTO YOUR STAND

'People watching' at shows is really very interesting - it's as if each stand has some kind of force-field surrounding it, stopping customers from stepping over the line and entering unknown territory! This is why making your brand engaging and having friendly staff is so important. For Zepter, we had a live cooking demonstration on the stand and hired promotional girls to encourage visitors to come in, watch and enter a competition. We also discovered that the French male assistant chef, Sebastian, was very good at attracting the ladies! Another approach is to have information on the outside of the stand, meaning visitors can learn about your brand before being 'jumped on' by the sales team. For Parago, we placed plasma screens facing outwards, allowing potential customers to find out more without having to actually walk onto the stand if they didn't want to.

On the other end of the scale, one tactic that virtually guarantees you'll be mobbed by visitors is giving away goody bags. And if you start early in the day and have the right give-aways, you'll find that within a few hours, your branded bags are all over the show or event.

An example of this working brilliantly was when we gave away exclusive VIP bags on Ladies' Day at the Newbury Races for Tuttoluxo, as part of their overall branding plan. The promotional girls were mobbed with onslaughts of women and hen parties (being VIP doesn't always mean they will act in a dignified manner!) The funniest and scariest part was when the organisers offered us the opportunity to cover another gate and, because we were short on promo girls, I put on the spare branded shirt and became a promo girl for the morning, along with the MD of Tuttoluxo! I'll never forget being mobbed by a huge group of 'hens' who were going mad for the goody bags as if it was life or death to get them - I nearly got trampled, but it was all good fun.

Although giving away freebies can be expensive and won't necessarily be the right thing to do at every event, if done correctly and in the right environment, it will help spread the word for your brand - and at Newbury it worked perfectly. Thousands of exclusive Tuttoluxo branded bags were given away at 9am...and by 9pm people were still walking around carrying them. Complementing this activity with radio and email campaigns, both running up to and after the event, really ensured the brand got the best exposure.

WHAT TO DO BEFORE, DURING AND AFTER A SHOW

With any campaign, you have to plan well, not only to ensure it runs as smoothly as possible, but also to allow time for more creative ideas to be explored, which will result in a better event.

Engaging with your audience prior to an event creates interest and hype and even if people can't actually attend the event, they've still had some

To ensure this animation is shown at it's best I recommend you hold the book open as flat as you can and hold your mobile device so the entire image is in view.

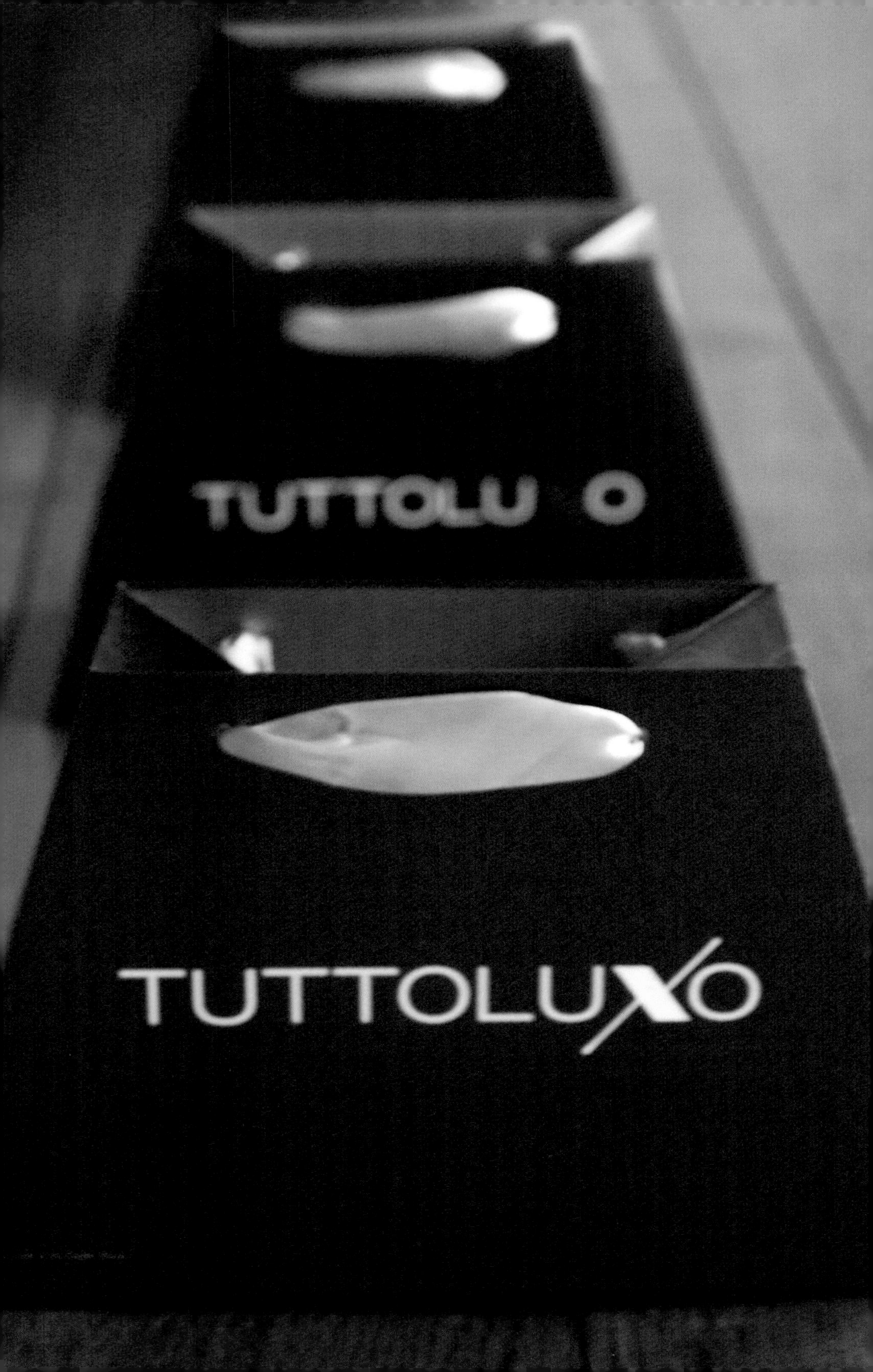
TUTTOLUXO

quality exposure to your brand. Using Tuttoluxo as an example, prior to every event some kind of competition or special offer would go out via all the social channels, on email and across their website. During the event, regular updates of what was happening and what celebrities had popped in for a massage were mentioned and all competition winners were photographed receiving their prize. Those photos were then sent out in an email and, again, across social networks after the event.

Although the Tuttoluxo promotions at the Cartier Polo and Sandbanks Polo only lasted one or two days, because of the promotional work done before and after, we ensured the campaign actually lasted a few weeks. Events like this are not cheap, so you need to maximise your exposure to make them worthwhile.

ENSURING EXTERNAL STAFF REPRESENT YOUR BRAND VALUES

If you're intending to hire extra staff (such as promotional boys and girls) for an event, it's advisable to interview them beforehand to ensure they fit with your brand. There's nothing worse than a high-end brand with a stylish stand having promotional staff who look and talk as though they're tempting customers into nightclubs! Once you've found the right staff, get a brief written up explaining what your brand is, your ethics and values and what's expected of them. If they need to understand the products in greater detail, then outline this in a document or give them a training session before the event begins. Once they're on your stand the public will assume they are a regular member of your team and will expect them to know about the brand.

With the Zepter stand, all the staff were given a written brief and details on the cookware prior to the event. They were also briefed in person the night before and were then given a demonstration on the morning of the show. The chefs were interviewed and given a demonstration on the unique characteristics of the products and were also given some cookware items to take away and experiment with, as they each needed to develop recipes that would not only demonstrate the characteristics, but would also be interesting to the public and easy enough to hand out on small plates for tastings.

TO FINISH OFF...

Here's a round-up of the key things you should do to make your presence felt at an exhibition or event and ensure your brand really stands out, before, during and after:

1. Research events thoroughly to find out whether they're right for your brand and where and how you need to have your stand

2. Work with a designer to come up with a stand system that maximises exposure of your brand while fitting within budget

3. Think about interesting and creative ways to encourage people to visit your stand and look at what give-aways and competitions might work

4. Come up with other ways to maximise your exposure at the show, through direct mail, email, social media and your website

5. Brief your staff properly and give them extra motivation to represent your brand in the best possible way – maybe sales incentives or a lovely dinner and drinks

6. Follow up after the event with further PR and marketing

MAKE YOUR BRAND A
TRULY SENSORY EXPERIENCE

WE CAN DISTINGUISH BETWEEN OVER 10,000 DIFFERENT SMELLS, EACH OF WHICH TRIGGERS DIFFERENT EMOTIONAL RESPONSES - THEY CAN MAKE US FEEL HAPPY, SAD, RELAXED AND EVEN BRING BACK CHILDHOOD MEMORIES. WE BREATHE 26,000 TIMES A DAY AND OUR SENSE OF SMELL IMPACTS OUR LIVES 24 HOURS A DAY.

BRANDS ALREADY TRIGGER OUR OTHER SENSES, FROM THE WAY THEIR LOGOS AND STORE LAYOUTS CATCH OUR EYE, TO THE WAY THEY DESCRIBE THEIR BUSINESS WITH WORDS AND IMAGES ON THEIR WEBSITE, THROUGH TO THE FEEL OF THE PAPER AND FINISH THEY USE ON THEIR BROCHURES. ENGAGING ALL THE SENSES CREATES A COMPLETELY IMMERSIVE CUSTOMER EXPERIENCE THAT HELPS TO FOSTER DEEPER EMOTIONAL BONDS BETWEEN YOUR BRAND AND YOUR AUDIENCE.

CAN YOU RECOGNISE THE UNIQUE SMELL OF CRAYOLA OR PLAY-DOH AS YOU OPEN THE PACKET, OR THE AROMA OF LUSH COSMETICS BEFORE YOU'VE EVEN SEEN THE SIGN FOR THE STORE? EACH IS AS INSTANTLY IDENTIFIABLE AS THE BRAND'S NAME AND LOGO AND ADDS SOMETHING EXTRA TO THE USUAL VERBAL AND VISUAL EXPERIENCE.

Using scent is nothing new - retailers have long been known to leverage atmospheric scent as a motivator. Bloomingdale's bathes its infant department in the scent of baby powder and some convenience stores have been known to use the aroma of coffee to persuade customers to go inside. But now more and more businesses are realising the power of scent and that bespoke fragrances can be created specifically for a brand.

A scent can even be patented - for example, 'cis-3-Hexenal', which is the smell of freshly cut grass, has been patented by a Dutch company and is used on tennis balls to remind people of Wimbledon.

More and more brands, from leading designer clothing labels to hotels, are now having unique scents created to heighten their customers' experiences. The intoxicating scent of a new car is key to connecting with a potential new owner, which has resulted in many car brands bottling this 'new car smell' and spraying it into new vehicles. In the United States, Cadillac infuses its cars' interiors with a custom scent called Nuance, to ensure that their models smell distinct from other vehicles.

SOME OTHER EXAMPLES:

Westin Hotels infuses a white tea fragrance throughout its lobbies. The signature fragrance was apparently chosen for 'its simplicity and its ability to both relax and energise'.

SONY infuses the scent of mandarin orange and vanilla in their stores and showrooms and is exploring methods to radiate the scent from store windows to entice shoppers with a whiff of a new flat screen, camera or laptop.

Singapore Airlines began distributing brand-scented towels nearly a decade and a half ago.

Swissotel in Berlin combined typical Swiss ingredients, luxurious components and 'Berlin smells' to create a scent that made people feel at home but at the same time had a local touch. The scent was used in the large lobby area and circulated through the air-conditioning.

The London-based shirt brand, PINK, scents its stores with a continuous spray of a proprietary 'line-dried linen' perfume.

Scents have even been created for car parks, usually dispersed near payment machines or staircases. The idea is to create a safe feeling for customers to make them more loyal.

VERY NICE, BUT CAN IT INCREASE REVENUE?

It's all very well using different techniques to make brands more interesting, engaging and memorable, but you need to ensure they add value and give you a bottom-line return at some point. Several studies have been conducted and have shown that ambient aromas can definitely impact consumer behaviour.

The neurologist and psychiatrist, Dr. Alan R. Hirsch, studied the effects of fragrance and found scent to be a highly effective motivator. He undertook a study at the Hilton in Las Vegas to see if the presence of fragrances would increase revenues and found that gamblers inserted 45.1% more coins into slot machines where a pleasant fragrance was added. At first, it seemed possible that the gamblers might simply have been attracted to the pleasant aroma and chosen the machines in those areas over other machines in the control group areas. However, the final results showed that not only did the scented areas receive more traffic, the slot machines in the fragrance-free areas showed zero decrease in revenue.

Research has also shown that scented products are considered both of higher value and better quality than unscented alternatives. That means not only could your product be perceived in a better light, but you may be able to increase its price! However, if you do go down the route of associating some kind of scent with your brand, you must test it thoroughly with your audience, as what might be pleasant to one person may be quite off-putting to another and you want your brand to have the right lasting impression.

Starbucks insists that staff do not wear any perfume, as it interferes with the aroma of the coffee. And, despite the added pressure to increase revenue, they actually stopped serving breakfast because the smell of eggs interfered with the coffee aroma. Although breakfast was supposed to have been a major growth product line, the reputation they had built around coffee was too fundamental to the business to risk damaging. Research shows that the majority of the good experience of drinking espresso comes from the coffee shop experience itself, so, in 2008, Starbucks decided to go back to grinding coffee in-store for the sole purpose of improving the aroma. Although pre-ground coffee is cheaper to transport, the management felt that any additional cost in that area would be offset by improved customer loyalty and higher sales.

THE RESULT IS IMMEDIATE: WHEN WE SMELL, WE FEEL.

C. RUSSELL BRUMFIELD, AUTHOR OF 'WHIFF!'

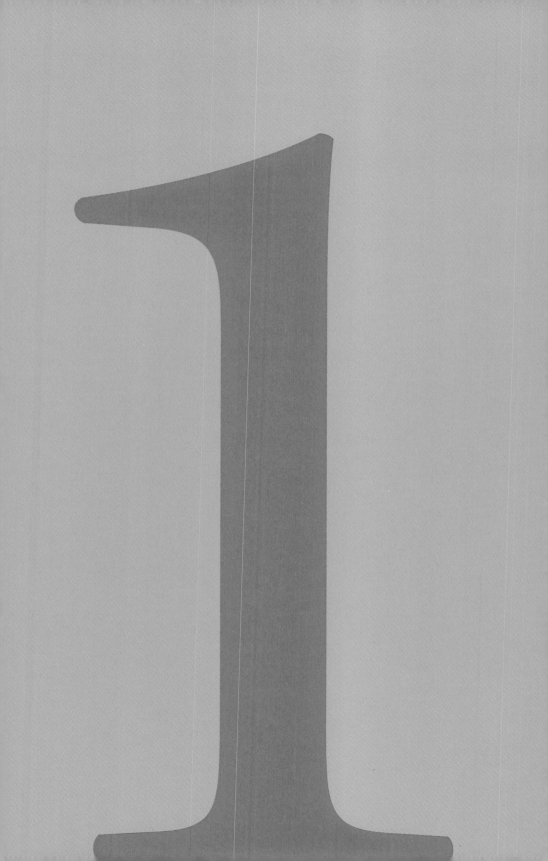

WORKING WITH AGENCIES TO DELIVER YOUR TOTAL BRAND EXPERIENCE

THE FIRST THING YOU NEED TO KNOW IS THAT EVERY AGENCY IS STRUCTURED DIFFERENTLY: SOME ARE 'FULL SERVICE', OFFERING EVERYTHING FROM CORPORATE IDENTITY TO DIGITAL, WHEREAS OTHERS SPECIALISE; SOME WILL ASSIGN YOU AN ACCOUNT HANDLER WHO WILL THEN MANAGE THE DESIGNERS, SOME ALLOW YOU TO SPEAK DIRECTLY TO THE DESIGNERS YOURSELF...AND SOME DON'T... AND SO ON. LARGE CORPORATES TEND TO HAVE SEVERAL AGENCIES, FROM THE WORLD-FAMOUS TO SMALLER INDEPENDENTS ON THEIR ROSTER. YOU MAY DECIDE TO ENGAGE SEPARATE AGENCIES FOR DIGITAL AND TRADITIONAL MEDIA, OR YOU MIGHT WANT IT ALL WITH ONE AGENCY.

However you decide to work, it's important that the agency/ies understand your brand and that you get on and can communicate well. As I mentioned at the start of the book, I don't believe you need to use an agency that specialises in your particular field; more often than not, an agency that doesn't know everything about your industry is better placed to look at your brand with fresh eyes and come up with some truly creative ideas.

If you want to have a campaign that is not only creative but will also require purchasing media space, you may have to engage the additional services of a media buying agency, as not all design agencies can offer both.

HOW TO BRIEF AN AGENCY

If you don't get this bit right from the start, you will end up wasting time and money. So, to ensure you get the best out of your design agency, you need to be very clear not only in giving them details on your brand, product or service and target audience, but also about what you want to achieve: is it increased revenue, brand awareness, a more user-friendly website, etc.? Any examples of ideas you have seen and liked, and brands you admire, will all help the agency gain a better understanding of your vision. At the same time, remember that you're engaging their services because you want something creative, so don't be too prescriptive!

I've worked with one-man bands to international companies and everything in between and, no matter how large or small they are, when projects get delayed it's always because of the same questions and issues. So here are a few of the main things you need to watch out for:

Have an approval process in place and one point of contact. When a design agency sends you a proof or design, make sure that all the appropriate people see and comment on the proof/design, but have one point of contact who can then compile this into one email or discuss it in one meeting with the design agency. I've had lots of experiences where several people from the same company keep sending contradictory comments through via email, which just gets messy and delays the process.

The same goes for copy. If you're providing copy for the agency, try to ensure that by the time you send it across, it has already been seen/approved by the relevant people. If the copy is in a near-perfect state, then it should just be a case of the odd tweak once it has been put in the design file. What clients often don't appreciate is that it's not just a case of cutting and pasting from one document to another – things such as line endings, orphans and widows have to be adjusted to fit the length and layout of the copy. I had one client who kept amending copy once it had been placed into the design and every time an amendment was made - such as lengthening/deleting a paragraph - the design had to be adjusted, which resulted in 14 rounds of different proofs being provided. And they were billed for it.

And, again, for websites! Make sure you check and understand everything to do with your website at the design stage. Once the approved designs and sitemap go to be coded, if you then want to make an adjustment to something - such as how the flow of navigation works - it will cost extra time and money to re-code.

Languages. Let the agency know from the start if the item will need to take into consideration different languages - this applies to both print and web. Different languages affect the total area required for the copy and some need to be read from right to left, which will affect page flow. Packaging has a limited space, so establishing early on how many languages and which languages will be used will save you money and time.

Deadlines. Always make deadlines clear to the agency. If you're attending an event in another country and need banners or an entire stand to be flown out, make sure this is accounted for in the process. And if one person within your company is the main contact for the agency, ensure they have a master file containing all the relevant information from the various departments/brands in the group so that the communication process can run smoothly.

THE TECHNICAL BITS

What is 'high res'? When working with anything printed, image files need to be submitted in high resolution. That means images need to be 300dpi (dots per inch) and over, which generally equates to a file size in excess of 1MB. If you're designing an exhibition stand or billboard, the larger the file size, the better.

Low res images are 72dpi. If you provide a low res image for print, it will generally print out pixelated, however low res images are used for the web because computer monitors display items at 72dpi.

Vector files. Logos are - or should be - created as a vector-based illustration using Illustrator or a similar programme, which allows you to enlarge a 1x1cm logo into something hundreds of meters larger without it pixelating. Logos created in Illustrator can be saved as an 'ai' or 'eps' file and these are the files you need to provide the agency with. They may only be a few KB in size, as they don't contain the same amount of information as an image. Creating a vector file means that your logo/graphic won't have a background and can therefore be placed on to anything without there being a white box behind it. If you don't currently have an eps or ai version of your logo, ask the person who created it to send you one immediately, otherwise it will cause issues in the future.

CMYK is a four-colour process used for printing. Rather than using a specific colour, the end colour is made up of a mix of cyan, magenta, yellow and black (known as 'key').

Pantone is a solid colour and is not mixed on the printer like CMYK. It's selected from the Pantone book and the specific ink is then purchased by the printer, all of which ensures your brand always has a consistent look with exactly the same colours (although different paper types can result in slight variations in the colour). If you're having branded clothing made, the specific Pantone coloured cotton dye can also be purchased.

RGB is the three-colour process used in the digital world - such as on televisions, computer monitors and mobile phones. It blends red, green and blue to display images, not CMYK. If a high-res image is provided in RGB but needs to be printed, an agency can convert this to CMYK for you.

Why does my logo look different on every computer and different to what's printed in our brochure? Printed materials will not always be exactly the same colour as you see on your computer screen, because of the different make-up of the colours (CMYK/RGB) and different types of paper and printing styles that can be used. Also, not every computer monitor is the same – in the same way that people have televisions of varying quality - so your website will not always look identical on every monitor.

Why can't I have a 6-page printed brochure? Literature is printed in sets of 4 pages - 4, 8, 12, and so on. If you take an A4 magazine that has been stitched or stapled down the centre and remove the staples, the pages will essentially be an A3 sheet that has been folded in half to create 4 pages.

Always check your proofs. Before any full order is printed, you will be sent either a pdf or a printed proof. Ensure you check everything, from the copy to the images, because once you confirm it's okay, the file will go to print and it's too late to make any adjustments. I've had a few proofs in the past that have been signed off by the client and then when I've completed a final design check (and I'm no copywriter!), I've found grammatical errors and spelling mistakes. You can't rely on a designer to get this aspect right, so make sure you proof the final version thoroughly, or it could be costly, not to mention embarrassing.

I'VE WORKED WITH EMMA FROM DAY
ONE OF SETTING UP MY BUSINESS, BACK
IN 2007. SHE NOT ONLY CREATED OUR
NATIONALLY - RECOGNISED BRAND, BUT
HAS ALWAYS BEEN THERE, EVEN WHEN
WE'VE HAD THE MOST RIDICULOUS
DEADLINES! SHE HAS ALWAYS STOOD
UP TO THE MARK AND ACHIEVED
EXCEPTIONAL RESULTS.

WITHOUT EMMA OUR BRAND WOULD
NOT BE WHAT IT IS TODAY.

STEVE BOLTON, FOUNDER, PLATINUM PROPERTY PARTNERS

AFTERWORD: ABOVE AND BEYOND...

Writing this book has been a very interesting journey for me. When I finally got around to putting down all of my experiences over the last few years and went back over the various brands and campaigns I'd worked on, I realised that, no matter what size, all those brands needed my help because of the same fundamental problem: they had forgotten that their brand was so much more than a logo.

It's so easy to get stuck in the continuous cycle of what's happening to your business on a day-to-day basis that you can easily forget to come up for air and take a look around. When you finally do, you suddenly realise how much everything has changed – and it's especially true nowadays with technology moving at such a phenomenal pace.

Taking a different approach and really getting back to the roots of 'who' your brand is and what it's trying to say can vastly improve not only external perceptions – like Tuttoluxo increasing UK revenue by 361% - but can also re-energise internal staff, as we saw with BankToTheFuture.com.

I hope I've given you a better understanding of not only what else is out there to help grow your brand, but also how important the foundations are and what value the right design agency can add to your business - because money and pretty pictures alone cannot create an unstoppable brand.

If you're going to implement any of the ideas I've written about, make sure you get the whole team behind you. With a great vision, good foundations and everyone working with commitment and consistency, you can't fail.

Finally, remember that a logo is not a brand; your logo is the symbol that represents everything your company is; your brand is everything you do and how you do it, and it needs to exemplify your vision and values.

LOVE YOUR BRAND...FROM START TO FINISH AND BEYOND.

ADVERTS · RADIO ·

EVENTS · TV · PAY PER CLICK

Online · BILLBOARDS · EXHIBITION STANDS ·

Banner · augmented Reality · ADVERTISING ·

FACEBOOK · MAGAZINES · APPS

Projection mapping...

QR CODE · Printed collateral

DIGITAL CHANNELS · CAMPAIGN

STORE AND OFFICE BRANDING · BRANDED MERCHANDISE · EMAIL · WEBSITE DESIGN ·

Social media · BROCHURE · stationary

BRANDED SCENTS · DIRECT MAIL

VIDEO

PACKAGING

TONE OF VOICE · competitors · WHAT TYPE OF BRAND

brand message · design · LOGO YOU

BRAND ARCHITECTURE

Remember the
brand foundations
and **have fun building
your skyscraper!**

ACKNOWLEDGEMENTS

I would like to thank...
My clients, all of whom have been a pleasure to work with, and
especially those who have allowed me to use their brands as examples.

Sarah Walker, my editor, for reading, re-reading and checking
my errors and making valuable suggestions.

I would also like to thank: Aurasma, especially Andrew Barclay and Christopher
Burges for their help and allowing me to use their technology; the typographic
legend Erik Spiekermann for replying to my twitter questions; Rob Shaw for
allowing me to use photography of the Jack Wills bag; Stuart Hogg for his imput
with the L'Oreal case study; Mike Harris and Chris Radford and Simon Dixon for
their invaluable suggestions; Victoria Kitchingman for the Dancing Kites Augmented
Reality animation; Madeline Ward from The Danse for the Parago 3D Augmented
reality; James Alliban for the video of his AR business card; TMW for their help
with the First Direct mail campaign information; Lyndsey O'dea for proofreading;
Mark Berry for his copywriting contribution; Mark Talmage-Rostron for copywriting
the Brand Blueprint advert; Steve Lane for Copyright and IP advice; John Cassidy
for my promotional shots; Bliss Dixon for promotional video and Claire McDonnell
for make-up.

PICTURE CREDITS

Every effort has been made to locate and credit copyright holders of the material
reproduced in this book. The author and publisher apologise for any omissions
and errors, which can be corrected in future editions.

AUGMENTED REALITY EXAMPLES

p95, p139, p140, p141, p153, p154, p155, p161, p162, p163, p164, p165, p169, p178

CREDITS

AUTHOR & DESIGNER OF BEYOND THE LOGO: E J CARTER

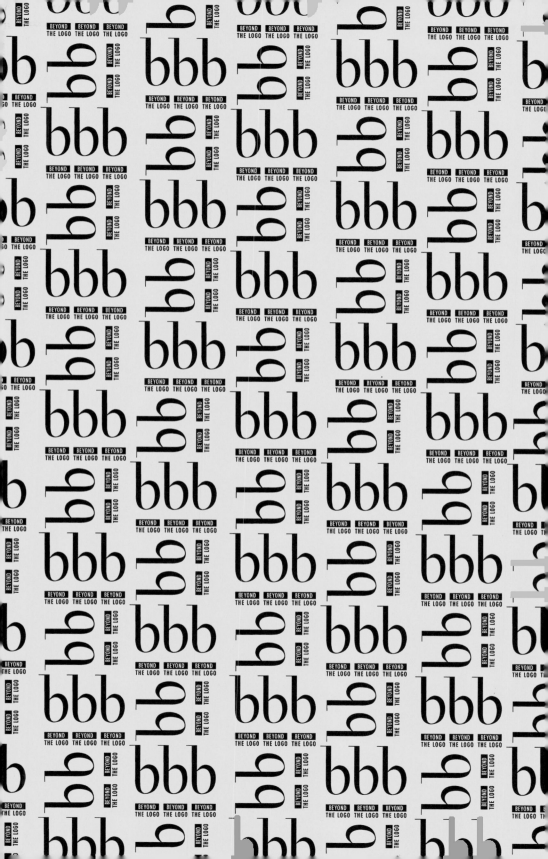

Lightning Source UK Ltd.
Milton Keynes UK
UKIC01n0033120116
266199UK00011B/107